DATE DUE

DEMCO 38-296

GREAT WRITERS OF THE ENGLISH LANGUAGE

American Classics

TAFF CREDITS

Executive Editor
Reg Wright

Series Editor
Sue Lyon

Editors
Jude Welton
Sylvia Goulding

Deputy Editors
Alice Peebles
Theresa Donaghey

Features Editors
Geraldine McCaughrean
Emma Foa
Ian Chilvers

Art Editors
Kate Sprawson
Jonathan Alden
Helen James

Designers
Simon Wilder
Frank Landamore

Senior Picture Researchers
Julia Hanson
Vanessa Fletcher
Georgina Barker

Picture Clerk
Vanessa Cawley

Production Controllers
Judy Binning
Tom Helsby

Editorial Secretaries
Fiona Bowser
Sylvia Osborne

Managing Editor
Alan Ross

Editorial Consultant
Maggi McCormick

Publishing Manager
Robert Paulley

Reference Edition Published 1989
Published by Marshall Cavendish Corporation
147 West Merrick Road
Freeport, Long Island
N.Y. 11520

Typeset by Litho Link Ltd., Welshpool
Printed and Bound in Italy by
L.E.G.O. S.p.a. Vicenza

LIBRARY OF CONGRESS
Library of Congress Cataloging-in-Publication Data
Great Writers of the English Language
    p. cm.
    Includes index vol.
    ISBN 1-85435-000-5 (set): $399.95
    1. English literature — History and criticism. 2. English
literature — Stories, plots, etc. 3. American literature — History
and criticism. 4. American literature — Stories, plots, etc.
5. Authors. English — Biography. 6. Authors. American — Biography.
I. Marshall Cavendish Corporation.
PR85.G66 1989
820'.9 – dc19   88-21077
                                                         CIP

ISBN 1–85435–000–5 (set)
ISBN 1–85435–007–2 (vol)

GREAT WRITERS OF THE ENGLISH LANGUAGE

American Classics

Mark Twain

F. Scott Fitzgerald

John Steinbeck

Ernest Hemingway

MARSHALL CAVENDISH · NEW YORK · TORONTO · LONDON · SYDNEY

CONTENTS

MARK TWAIN

⟶ *1835-1910* ⟵

Samuel Langhorne Clemens led a life as packed with adventure as
any of his stories. The characters he met, the hazards he faced, the
voices he heard, the wry conclusions he reached about human nature
were all distilled into a series of books which made him a worldwide
celebrity. The man himself was well suited to such acclaim – a giant
personality who delighted in the fame his scathing humour brought
him. His home country now dubs him the keystone of great
American literature.

A Popular Hero

From the backwoods of Missouri, printer and river-pilot Sam Clemens rose to worldwide fame for his hilarious, irreverent stories of American life – written under the pseudonym 'Mark Twain'.

When Samuel Clemens was 25 years old a clairvoyant told him 'You write well but are rather out of practice. No matter, you will be *in* practice some day.' These were to prove prophetic words for a man who, although a river pilot at the time, was to write some of the best-loved – and best-selling – books of American literature, and which now rank among the greatest masterpieces of all time.

Samuel Langhorne Clemens – better known as Mark Twain – was born on 30 November 1835 in a village called Florida, in Monroe County, Missouri. His father, John Marshall Clemens, was a lawyer who had moved West from Tennessee in the hope of making his fortune in the developing frontier country. It was not to be an easy time for him or for his family. Sam, the sixth of seven children, was born two months prematurely. As he wrote in his *Autobiography*, 'I was a sickly and precarious and tiresome and uncertain child and lived mainly on allopathic medicines during the first seven years of my life.' But the sickly child was to survive until well into his seventies.

When young Sam was four, Judge Clemens (as he was generally known) moved to the town of Hannibal on the west bank of the Mississippi. It was here that Sam grew up and where his imagination was captured by the romance of river life. Judge Clemens kept a grocery store as well as practising law, and he also tried his luck at other ventures such as slave trading. But he was not the success he had dreamed of being, and by the time he died in 1847, the family was virtually bankrupt. Sam took various part-time jobs and, at the age of 12, with his schooling officially ended, he was apprenticed to a printer.

Sam's brother Orion (ten years his senior) was also a printer, and in 1851 Sam went to work on his paper, the Hannibal *Journal*. As well as looking after the typesetting, Sam began writing humorous sketches of the kind that were then enormously popular, and in 1852 one of them was published in a Boston comic weekly called *The Carpet-Bag*; in old age he remarked that seeing his first literary efforts in print brought him 'a joy which rather exceeded anything in that line I have ever experienced since'.

TRAVELLING MAN

In 1853, at the age of 17, Sam decided to see something of the world, and for the next four years he worked as a journeyman printer, plying his trade wherever the mood took him. New York was his first port of call. From there he travelled to Philadelphia in the East, as well as to St Louis, Missouri and smaller towns such as Keokuk, Iowa.

His life as a printer was mainly one of drudgery, but it had its compensations in that it made up for his lack of formal schooling. 'One isn't a printer for ten years', he later recalled, 'without setting up acres of good and bad literature, and learning – unconsciously at first, consciously later – to discriminate between the two.'

'A sunshiny disposition'
Despite such glowing tributes which Twain paid to his mother (above) in his Autobiography, *Jane Clemens inflicted on her son a hell-fire Christianity which made him – like his father – reject religion.*

Mining days
(above) Sam dreamed of striking it rich. But his attempts at silver mining during the Civil War provided him with no money – although they did furnish him with the raw material for a book, Roughing It.

Humble beginnings
(left) Twain's birthplace in Florida, Missouri, was a ramshackle cottage. And the family fortunes continued to decline throughout his childhood.

New York printer
(left) 'I have taken a liking to the abominable place', Sam wrote home from New York. At 18, with years of apprenticeship behind him, he grubbed a tedious living there. Later he was to return in triumph.

Elder brother
(below) Orion gave Sam his early jobs on local publications in Hannibal. The brothers conspired in various wild schemes, but Orion eventually rose to the eminently respectable position of Secretary of Nevada Territory.

Mark Twain Memorial, Hartford, CT

Key Dates

1835 born Florida, Missouri

1848 apprentice printer

1857 river-pilot

1865 *Jumping Frog* published

1870 marries Olivia Langdon

1876 *Tom Sawyer*

1884 founds publishing company

1885 *Huckleberry Finn*

1894 goes bankrupt

1895 world lecture tour

1904 wife dies

1910 dies Connecticut

In 1856 Sam left Keokuk with the idea of making his fortune in South America. But en route he met Horace Bixby, a celebrated river pilot, whom he persuaded to teach him his trade. For the next four years this was Sam's life, first of all as Bixby's 'cub', learning the intricacies of the 1200-mile stretch of the Mississippi from St Louis to New Orleans, and then from 1859 as a registered pilot. It was a boyhood dream come true. During this time, Sam's literary career, such as it was, came to a virtual stop, but the four years he spent on the river stocked his mind with the colourful characters who were later to adorn his books. His pen-name 'Mark Twain' derives from the words called out when taking soundings from the bow of a river steamboat. (It indicates that the water is two fathoms – 12 feet – deep.)

PILOT AND WRITER

The outbreak of the Civil War in 1861 put an end to this happy period of Sam Clemens' life. His home state, Missouri, was on the border between North and South, and Sam's actions during the early days of the conflict reflect the uncertainty that was common at the time. In June 1861 he was very briefly a volunteer second lieutenant in a band of Confederate (Southern) militia, and during this dispiriting time he said he learned more about retreating 'than the man that invented retreating'. He switched his allegiance to the Union (Northern) side but abandoned his part in direct conflict. Instead he joined his brother Orion in Nevada.

There was money to be made in this virgin territory, but Sam was unlucky. His attempts at timber dealing and silver mining met with little success. But his experiences enriched *Roughing It* (1872), one of the classic accounts of the pioneering days of the West. It was writing that proved a life-line for Sam during these difficult days. He had been contributing sketches to a local newspaper, the Virginia City *Territorial Enterprise*, and in the summer of 1862 he was offered a job as a reporter on it. He walked more than 100 miles to take the job, and it was in the *Enterprise*, on 3 February 1863, that he first used his pen-name Mark Twain.

'Mark Twain' soon made a name for himself locally, and within a year of starting his job he wrote to his mother: 'I am prone to boast of having the widest reputation as a local editor of any man on the Pacific coast.' However, he deflated the apparent arrogance by adding at the end, 'And I am proud to say I am the most conceited ass in the Territory.' But his career on the *Enterprise* was to be short-lived. He was in the habit of writing hoax articles, and in 1864 one of them backfired. In an editorial that he wrote as a private joke, he made some tasteless remarks about miscegenation (the interbreeding of Blacks and Whites); it somehow got into print, and he was obliged to leave.

For a while Twain worked as a reporter on the *Morning Call* in San Francisco, then he made another attempt at mining. Again it was unsuccessful, but it was in a mining camp that he heard a tale that was to help make his reputation. It was about a prize jumping frog. Twain wrote a story based on it, entitled *Jim Smiley and his Jumping Frog,* that was published in the New York *Saturday Press* on 18 November 1865 and in other newspapers soon afterwards. The story marked a turning point in his career – at the age of 30 he had suddenly 'arrived' as an author.

AN ENGAGING DRAWL

Despite the success of the *Jumping Frog* story, the beginning of 1866 marked a low point for Twain. He was hard up, was imprisoned for drunkenness and at one stage contemplated suicide. But in March he was sent to Hawaii as a correspondent for the Sacramento *Union.* His account of a disaster at sea – the burning of the clipper ship *Hornet* – won him a new reputation as a serious reporter, and on his return he embarked on a highly successful career as a lecturer. His voice had an engaging drawl and he was an even more skilful performer with the spoken word than he was on the printed page. According to people who heard him, he made audiences laugh until they were too weak to leave their seats. Inspired by his success, he made a tour of the Mediterranean in 1867, recording his impressions in a series of letters published in 1869 as *The Innocents Abroad.* With this book, in which he poked fun at foreign foibles and pretensions, he became the most widely read author in America.

The Mediterranean trip had another important consequence in Twain's life. One of his fellow passengers was Charles Langdon, a young man from a rich New York family. Twain fell in love with a picture of Langdon's sister Olivia (Livy) – a reaction confirmed when he met the original that Christmas in New York. She was gentle, affectionate and beautiful, but was less than susceptible to Twain's own qualities. She rejected his proposal, disapproving of his smoking and drinking

T. Frere: Empress Eugenie visiting the Pyramids/Christie's/Bridgeman Art Library

Love at first sight

Twain was captivated by a picture of Olivia Langdon (right). It took 200 letters to win her, and with their marriage began a relationship which has enthralled critics ever since. Was she a taming influence on her free-thinking husband? Did she nag him into a narrower frame of mind? Did she lessen the satirical impact of Twain's greatest books? Or was she the bedrock security and source of domestic peace which actually enabled him to achieve masterpieces? Her husband called her 'the real fortune of my life'.

Mark Twain Memorial, Hartford, CT

FRONTIER HUMOUR

Among the American humorists who flourished at the same time as Mark Twain, was Bret Harte (1836–1902). Both men worked on Californian newspapers in the 1860s, and Twain acknowledged that Harte 'trimmed and trained and schooled me from an awkward utterer of coarse grotesqueness to a writer of paragraphs and chapters'. But Twain came to detest Harte, calling him 'a liar, a thief, a snob, a sot, a sponge, a coward'. When Harte was appointed consul in Germany, Twain condemned sending 'this nasty creature to puke upon the American name in a foreign land'. But Harte's career survived.

Mary Evans Picture Library

Family home
(above) At the height of his financial success, Twain designed Nook Farm in Hartford. A folly of a house inspired by a Mississippi steamboat, it was a symbol of success and a haven from a society in turmoil.

Not-so-innocent abroad
In 1867 Twain undertook a five-month cruise to Europe and the Middle East (left). He made comic capital from foreign 'foibles' in his popular book The Innocents Abroad.

was busy. He enjoyed playing host in the splendid mansion he had built in 1874 – one room was designed to look like the pilot-house of a steamer. It cost more than $125,000, but Twain could afford this kind of extravagance while his career was flourishing.

RICH MAN, POOR MAN . . .

There have been few authors who knew more about the whole process of making books than Mark Twain, and because he generally did not trust publishers he set up his own publishing firm in 1884. It was called Charles L. Webster and Company, a nephew of that name being nominally in charge. Twain started his publishing career with an astonishing coup. Ulysses S. Grant, the Union commander in the Civil War and the 18th President of the United States, had gone bankrupt and saw the publication of his memoirs as the only way of saving his family from penury. Twain correctly foresaw that the *Memoirs* would have a huge sale and offered a much better deal than other publishers, in order to secure them for his company.

They were published in two volumes in autumn 1885, a few months after Grant's death. More than 200,000 sets were sold; Charles Webster and Company made a profit of over $200,000. In the same year, Twain's firm published his masterpiece, *The Adventures of Huckleberry Finn*, and the controversy it aroused helped to ensure its success.

Twain's business instinct was not always infallible, however, and an expensive indulgence in a pet scheme led to his downfall. As a former typesetter, he was fascinated by the process, and in the 1880s he became involved with an inventor named James W. Paige, who was developing a typesetting machine that, with one operator at its keyboard, could do the work of four men setting type by hand. It was a marvellous piece of machinery, but its thousands of separate parts made it impossibly delicate. Twain poured money into the Paige machine, and by 1891 was in serious financial trouble. That year he closed his Hartford home in an effort to economize, and moved to Europe with his family. He made return visits to America to save the situation, but his efforts were to no avail. In 1894 he was declared bankrupt, with nearly $100,000 still owing.

Frog leap to fame
(above) Twain won fame with Jim Smiley *and his* Jumping Frog. *It epitomizes 'frontier humour', also practised by Bret Harte (left).*

and hostility towards institutionalized religion. It took two years and over 200 letters from Twain to Livy before they were eventually married in February 1870.

With the exception of his marriage, 1870 was a bad year for Mark Twain. His father-in-law died of cancer, and Livy, after a near-miscarriage, gave birth to a premature, sickly baby boy who was to die before he was two. They had been living in Buffalo, where Twain had bought an interest in a newspaper, during this trying period, and he decided on a move to get away from the scene of his unhappiness. In 1871 he and his family moved to Hartford, Connecticut, and Twain settled down to life as a professional writer.

During the 1870s Twain's reputation was consolidated with the publication of both non-fiction, *Roughing It*, and fiction, *The Adventures of Tom Sawyer*. Indeed, he had become so famous by 1872 that when *Roughing It* appeared, it sold 62,000 copies within four months. He also carried on his career on the lecture platform, delighting audiences not only in America but also in England, which he first visited in 1872. He had originally intended writing a satirical travel book about England, but he was so warmly received wherever he went that he became a confirmed anglophile.

Back in Hartford, Connecticut, Twain's social life

Enforced exile

Driven by impending bankruptcy to close up his house and live as cheaply as possible while paying off his debts, Twain took his family to Europe. They lived for a time in Berlin (right). Twain had something derisory to say about every foreign country he visited, except England, where he was welcomed so warmly. During these years of exile, he drove himself to exhaustion giving lectures to raise the money he needed.

F. Machatscheck: Berlin at Dusk/Fine Art Photographic Library

Twain was shattered by the failure of the cherished machine, but he refused to be beaten. He decided to undertake a worldwide reading tour in order to pay back every cent he owed. In the summer of 1895 he set off. He was now just a few months short of his 60th birthday, but he worked with enormous energy on the tour, which took him to Australia, New Zealand, India, Ceylon and South Africa. Audiences flocked to see him, and by 1898 he was solvent again.

PERSONAL TRAGEDY

Twain's public triumph was, however, marred by private grief. Arriving back in England in 1896 he received a cable from Connecticut saying that his eldest daughter, Susy, was ill; she had meningitis. Before the family could reach her, she died. Twain's brother, Orion, died the following year, and his wife and his youngest daughter, Jean, became chronic invalids.

In 1900 Twain returned to the United States a hero.

He embodied the American dream – someone who from humble beginnings had achieved unprecedented fame and fortune; someone who was true to himself and spoke his mind no matter what people thought of him – 'When in doubt, tell the truth' he was known to have said. Easily recognized with his mane of white hair, he was greeted rapturously and applauded wherever he went. People loved him; universities honoured him. Yale conferred on him a Master's degree in 1888 and then a doctorate in literature in 1901. And in 1907 came an honour from abroad – the prestigious Oxford University also conferred on him a doctorate. He quipped 'I don't know why they should give me a degree like that, I never doctored any literature. I wouldn't know how.' But he was thrilled, and commented that he would gladly have travelled to Mars and back, if necessary, to pick up his degree.

In 1901 Twain had written to a friend, 'I am approaching the threshold of age . . . This is no time to

'A broken-hearted family'

(left) The charming contentment of the Clemens family (from left to right, Clara, Livy, Jean, Sam and Susy) ended sadly. Livy became an invalid, Jean an epileptic and Susy died of meningitis. A baby son died, too. When Livy succumbed to heart disease her husband wrote that his loss 'would bankrupt the vocabularies of all the languages to put it into words'.

Mark Twain Memorial, Hartford, CT

Mark Twain Memorial, Hartford, CT

Man of letters
(left) A man of backwoods education (and none at all beyond the age of 12) Mark Twain derived the greatest satisfaction from the honours heaped on him by academic institutions in later life. The degree conferred on him by Oxford University in 1907 both thrilled and amused him. It was the last ray of light to shine on his sad old age.

be flitting about the earth. I must cease from the activities proper to youth and begin to take on the dignities and gravities and inertia proper to honorable senility' and a few years later he started writing his autobiography. By now he was suffering from heart trouble and his health was poor, though to allay gloomy newspaper rumours (for fear Clara should read them in Europe and be upset) he telephoned Associated Press and denied that he was dying: 'I would never do such a thing at my time of life'. Living with his daughter, Jean, at Stormfield in Connecticut (his beloved Livy having died several years before), he avowed that the two of them would now be a family.

FINAL CHAPTER

But it was not to be. Jean, an epileptic, had a seizure and died just before Christmas in 1909, and Twain, heartbroken, realized that her death was to be the final chapter in his life: 'I shall never write any more.'

Twain recalled that Halley's comet, which appears at intervals of 75 years, had been in the skies when he was born and said it would be 'the greatest disappointment of my life' if he failed to go out with it. Four months later he had his last wish, for the comet reappeared, blazing in the night sky when, on 21 April 1910, Mark Twain quietly died.

Fact or Fiction

HICK TOWN

Hannibal, Missouri, where Sam Clemens grew up, stood on the shores of the Mississippi, with forests and hills on its doorstep and the promise of camping, fishing, swimming and adventure all around. It haunted Twain's imagination all life long and was the basis for St Petersburg in *Tom Sawyer* and *Huckleberry Finn*, and Dawson's Landing in *Pudd'nhead Wilson*. At nine, he witnessed a local murder, and recreated it in *Huckleberry Finn* when Huck sees the murder of a harmless drunk. Portraying hick-town America (below) was his true forte. When Twain visited Hannibal in later life (he last went there in 1902) he experienced a great degree of 'pathos' and a helpless longing for the lost Eden of his boyhood.

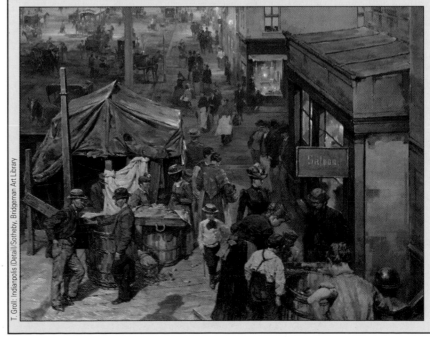

T. Groll: Indianpolis (Detail)/Sotheby, Bridgeman Art Library

THE ADVENTURES OF HUCKLEBERRY FINN

In this riotous tale of a skittish young boy and his endearing companion, Twain makes a powerful plea for the liberation of 'natural and healthy instincts' suppressed by Southern society.

At once a comedy, an adventure story and an incisive moral protest, *The Adventures of Huckleberry Finn* can be enjoyed at several levels. Recounted by a bright and mischievous 13-year-old boy, the novel owes its unique flavour to Twain's rejection of 'British English' in favour of the rich dialects of the American South. The result is a narrative which is deceptively artless in its appeal, harbouring an ironic cutting edge.

Against the innocent enthusiasm of Huck setting off on his journey down the Mississippi, Twain poses a world where corruption and exploitation are rife. Huck's episodic contact with this world lends the novel its buoyant humour. And his conflict with it allows Twain to explore the dilemma of the individual caught between his own desire for freedom and the demands of society at large.

GUIDE TO THE PLOT

Huck introduces himself as Tom's comrade from the *The Adventures of Tom Sawyer* by "Mr Mark Twain". That tale ended with the two boys discovering a robbers' hoard of gold, and sharing it as a reward. Huck is now living with the Widow Douglas, who has taken him in "for her son, and allowed she would sivilize me".

Huck's new clothes make him feel "all cramped up", and he can see no sense in the spelling or Bible lessons he has to endure. When he hears about "the bad place . . . I said I wished I was there. She got mad, then, but I didn't mean no harm. All I wanted was to go somewheres; all I wanted was a change, I warn't particular". Huck's only solace is to sneak out at night to meet Tom Sawyer, and plot imaginary adventures.

But real adventures are close at hand. Just as Huck begins to get "sort of used to the Widow's ways", his father (pap), a mean and drunken reprobate, turns up, eager to get his hands on Huck's money. He kidnaps Huck, locking him up in a cabin in the woods. Huck's relief at returning to a life of ease – smoking, fishing and "cussing" – is offset by his pap's cruelty, and he resolves to escape. He concocts an elaborate pretence that he has been murdered and slips down river in a canoe.

At nearby Jackson's Island, Huck meets Jim, a runaway slave who belongs to Miss Watson, the Widow Douglas' sister. "I bet I was glad to see him," says Huck and the two fugitives team up. Having sworn Huck to secrecy, Jim tells him that he has run away because he overheard that Miss Watson was planning to sell him down the river (where he

L. Suthers: Dame Trimmer/Whitford and Hughes/Bridgeman Art Library

Wreck ahoy!
(left) Huck and Jim encounter a wrecked steamer "mournful and lonesome in the middle of the river". Huck drags a reluctant Jim on board to explore, only to surprise a pair of potential murderers.

Southern refinement
(right) Huck's stay with the handsome, aristocratic Grangerford family, gives him an unaccustomed taste of hospitality – "And warn't the cooking good, and just bushels of it too!"

R. Casas: Interior in the Open Air (Detail), Marques de Villamizar/Bridgeman Art Library

F. Remington: The Winchester/Christies, Bridgeman Art Library

"Kill them!"
(above) Huck is witness to a shoot-out between the Grangerfords and a rival family. It makes him wish "I hadn't ever come ashore that night, to see such things".

P. Hurd: Sermon from Revelations, The Corcoran Gallery of Art, Washington DC

The 'king' at work
(left) At a prayer meeting, the con-man known as 'the king' poses as a reformed pirate. His 'performance' earns him "eighty-seven dollars and seventy-five cents".

"A poor lost lamb"
(left) The well-meaning Widow Douglas tries to smooth Huck into an acceptable shape – but her "dismal regular and decent" ways fret him as much as his new clothes.

would suffer the appalling fate of working in the cotton fields with no hope of being reunited with his family). Huck and Jim hide on Jackson's Island for a few days before setting off on a raft for Cairo, the junction with the Ohio river that led to the free states.

However, they unwittingly float past Cairo, and are separated when their raft is overturned by a steamboat. Huck swims ashore and reaches the house of an aristocratic Southern family, the Grangerfords. They welcome him warmly, and he makes friends with Buck, the youngest son. Huck thinks them "a mighty nice family" – until he learns they are engaged in a bitter feud with the rival Shepherdson family. The feud soon erupts into a shoot-out in which Buck's father and his two brothers are killed. Sickened and scared, Huck escapes and rediscovers Jim and the raft – and is, understandably, "powerful glad to get away from the feuds".

Huck's idyllic life on the river with Jim is

again interrupted, however. They meet two professional frauds, one posing as the Duke of Bridgewater, the other as the "son of Looy the Sixteenth and Marry Antonette". Huck soon wises up to these "low-down humbugs", but he and Jim accommodate them on the raft. The two con-men meanwhile pursue various plans to trick the folk of the riverside towns out of as much money as possible.

> "We said there warn't no home like a raft, after all. Other places do seem so cramped up and smothery, but a raft don't. You feel mighty free and easy and comfortable on a raft."

After setting up a farcical "Shaksperean Revival", the duke hears about the death of a wealthy landowner, who had been expecting the arrival of his two brothers from England. With Huck acting as their 'valet', the duke and king set about convincing the dead man's daughters and friends that they are the brothers. But they overreach themselves, and their scheme ends in mayhem. Huck narrowly escapes his unfair share of the towns-folks' retribution and rejoins Jim who has stayed in hiding.

Huck's joy at the reunion is immediately ruined by the appearance of the king and duke, fleeing the town to the safety of the raft. Penniless once more, they resort to their old tricks – and one new plan. Behind Huck's back, they sell Jim to a local farmer "for forty dirty dollars"; but Huck, against his own 'conscience' determines to find and free Jim.

He discovers that the farmer is none other than Tom Sawyer's uncle, and that he and his wife are expecting a visit from Tom himself. When Tom arrives, he organizes a complicated series of storybook pranks to free Jim, who is chained up in an ouside hut. But their plans are discovered, and Tom finally reveals a vital piece of information that is to bring happiness to both Huck and Jim.

A COMIC ADVENTURE
Huckleberry Finn is a comic novel whose humour depends largely on the character of its hero-narrator. Endearingly honest and fresh in his outlook, Huck can spot the absurd side of any situation. He is also intrinsically comic in his natural antipathy to the convention-ridden world of adulthood:

After supper she got out her book and learned me about Moses and the Bulrushers; and I was in a sweat to find out all about him; but by-and-by she let it out that Moses had been dead a considerable time; so then I didn't care no more about him; because I don't take no stock in dead people.

13

Reader's Guide

At other times, the novel's wit works on the level of slapstick or farce, climaxing in the episode where the king and duke pose as a dead man's heirs. In these hilarious charlatans, with their gaudy clothes, absurd pretensions and consuming greed, Twain realized his genius for comic burlesque. For example, the duke tries to teach the king Hamlet's soliloquy for their "Shaksperean Revival". But the duke's memory is a little dim: "*To be, or not to be; that is the bare bodkin/That makes calamity of so long life;/For who would fardels bear, till Birnam Wood do come to Dunsinane . . .*" However, the parody does not obscure the fact that – as Huck perceives – these men are avaricious swindlers who deceitfully live off the gullibility of others.

HUCK'S INWARD JOURNEY

The great theme of the novel is Huck's growth in moral perception, which involves his rejection of the values society has tried to instill in him. Huck's developing relationship with Jim forms the moral core of the novel. His acceptance of the Southern attitude to 'niggers' – inherent in its legal and social codes – is challenged by his growing realization that Jim is a true friend and ally – indeed, his only one. He repeatedly feels duty-bound to reveal Jim's identity as a runaway slave, but is always held back by Jim's kindness and integrity.

Huck's inner conflict reaches a crisis when he recalls how he had been taught at Sunday School "that people that acts as I'd been acting about that nigger goes to everlasting fire". Conscience-stricken, Huck resolves to write a letter home, telling Miss Watson of Jim's whereabouts. But no sooner has he done it,

G. Caleb Bingham: The County Election/Saint Louis Art Museum

T. Moran: Slaves escaping Through the Swamp. (Detail) Philbrook Museum of Art, Tulsa, OK

In the Background

FLIGHT FROM SLAVERY

In the years preceding the American Civil War, many slaves tried to escape to the free states of the North. Jim's flight is unaided (apart from Huck's moral and practical support), but many runaways were helped by ardent abolitionists who gave them food and shelter. They also set up an 'Underground Railway', whereby runaways could reach the safety of Canada. At the time that *Huckleberry Finn* is set – at least 30 years before the Civil War – it was an offence under Southern law to give such aid to runaway slaves. Huck's final commitment to free Jim therefore not only places him beyond the pale of Southern society, but makes him, too, an outlaw.

A runaway slave *risked pursuit and punishment by outraged Southerners, until the boundary to the free states was crossed.*

F. McCubbin: The Yarra: Studley Park/Christies, Brdgeman Art Library

than he remembers how Jim "would always call me honey, and pet me, and do everything he could think of for me, and how good he always was". In the novel's most ironic moment, he tears up the letter – "all right then, I'll *go* to hell" – and chooses the "wickedness" of loyalty and humanity over the 'virtues' of profit and betrayal.

This moving scene relates to another recurrent theme. Just as Huck is torn between his own, intuitive values and those of society, so the freedom and beauty of the countryside is

> "**I** *would take up wickedness again, which was in my line, being brung up to it, and the other warn't. And for a starter, I would go to work and steal Jim out of slavery again;*"

contrasted with the "sivilized" world which is overrun with violence and greed. All the adults Huck knows – except Jim – from his father to Miss Watson to the king and duke, are guilty to a greater or lesser extent. And his positive delight in the free and easy life on the raft, indicates an instinctive desire for a gentle and uncorrupt way of living, not to be found among any of the Mississippi towns he visits.

Set among Huck and Jim's hectic adventures, the quiet moments on the raft gain in poignancy, for it is then that Huck's moral education is taking place, and his natural aversion to hypocrisy, self-interest and materialism is nurtured.

A public auction
(above) Passing themselves off as a dead man's brothers, the king and his friend the duke have the "out-and-out cheek" to have his effects auctioned off – with a view to pocketing the proceeds.

Reunited again
(left) Fate lands Huck at the farm of Tom Saywer's uncle, just as his erstwhile comrade is paying a visit there. Tom evolves a complicated plan to free Jim, who is chained up in an outside hut, and the two boys set to work with a will (right).

CHARACTERS IN FOCUS

The characters in *Huckleberry Finn*, be they pious or reprobate, all play a part in Huck's journey, helping to drive him away from dry land and continue his life on the raft. Mostly grasping or hypocritical, they reflect Twain's hatred of the base values of the American South, but are rich in the realism of raw Mississippi life. Twain gives his characters a variety of Deep South dialects, including those common to negro slaves and backwoods folk, with which he had a 'personal familiarity'.

WHO'S WHO

Huckleberry Finn Hero and narrator, a shrewd, quick-witted 13-year-old boy, who finds life with genteel folks "tiresome and lonesome".

Jim A runaway Negro slave, and an unexpected but natural companion for Huck on his journey down river. Jim's unaffected kindness and sympathy are crucial in forming Huck's moral ideas.

"The old man" Huck's father. A greedy, reprehensible drunkard – "every time he got drunk he raised Cain around town; and every time he raised Cain he got jailed . . . this kind of thing was right in his line."

Tom Sawyer Huck's only friend in the painfully respectable world of St Petersburg, Missouri. Tom's adventures are, unlike Huck's, pure make-believe – the stuff of "pirate books".

The Grangerford Family An aristocratic Southern family who live in a "mighty nice house" in real "style", and temporarily shelter Huck.

The king and duke A pair of outrageous con-men whom Huck and Jim allow to share their raft. Huck quickly sums them up as "frauds", but "I never said nothing, never let on . . . it's the best way . . ." Huck and Jim's tolerance is repaid with riotous entertainment – and finally treachery.

Silas and Sally Phelps Tom Sawyer's uncle ("the innocentest, best old soul") and aunt, whose farm is the setting for Huck and Tom's final pranks together.

W. Homer: The Nooning, Wadsworth Atheneum, Hartford. The Ella Gallup Sumner and Mary Catlin Sumner Coll.

J. Wingate: Poachers; Fine Art Society/Bridgeman Art Library.

Unprepossessing in appearance, the self-styled king and duke (left) have an astonishing range of talents designed to con the all-too-gullible townsfolk along the Mississippi. The duke describes himself as a "theatre-actor – tragedy, you know; take a turn at mesmerism and phrenology when there's a chance; teach singing-geography school for a change"; while the king's specialities are "doctoring", fortune-telling, preaching and "missionaryin around".

"*Living in a house, and sleeping in a bed, pulled on me pretty tight, mostly*", writes Huck (left). His decision to head down river is very much a natural choice, and his ensuing encounters with Southern townsfolk involve him in, at best, farce, and at worst, danger, confirming his instinct that "it's lovely to live on a raft".

The runaway slave Jim is Huck's loyal friend and ally, with whom he spends his most free and peaceful moments on the raft (right) – "We had the sky, up there, all speckled with stars, and we used to . . . look up at them, and discuss about whether they was made, or only just happened . . ." Huck's crisis of conscience over whether he should do the legally correct thing and betray Jim as a runaway evokes a vivid memory of "Jim before me . . . in the day, and in the night-time, sometimes moonlight, sometimes storms, and we a floating along, talking, and singing, and laughing." Jim's constancy and good nature lead Huck to formulate his own humane (albeit illegal) set of values.

Huck's father (below) "was most fifty and he looked it". Mean and degenerate, he wants to show "who was Huck Finn's boss" – and does it by hiding Huck away while he fights a lawsuit to get hold of the boy's money. His natural aggression is aggravated by frequent drinking bouts, when he berates the "govment" for allowing the law "to take a man's son away from him . . . which he has had all the trouble and all the anxiety and all the expense of raising".

"*Mary Jane* (right) *was* red-headed, but . . . she was most awful beautiful." She and her sisters are the most innocent victims of the king and duke's wiles. But Mary Jane participates with spirit in Huck's plan to expose the two "rapscallions", thereby earning his accolade, "she *was* the best girl I ever see".

ROUGH HUMOUR

Mark Twain claimed that he learned to write by printing other people's stories, but his biting brand of humour was entirely and irrepressibly his own.

Mark Twain was late in discovering his literary vocation, and despite his early talent for squibs and sketches, he was driven to write as a professional by sheer necessity. Stranded in Nevada, he informed his brother that 'The fact is, I must have something to do, and that *shortly*, too, even writing' – after which he took his first regular job as a journalist with the Virginia City *Territorial Enterprise*.

Three years later, Twain wrote, 'I have a "call" to literature, of a low order – *i.e.* humorous. It is nothing to be proud of, but it is my strongest suit.' From now on he would be 'seriously scribbling to excite the *laughter* of God's creatures. Poor, pitiful business!'

TALL TALES

In describing humour as literature 'of a low order', Mark Twain was only expressing a widely held opinion. The genteel tradition was strong in American writing, and humorous stories – especially stories written in dialect or common speech – tended to be undervalued, even by readers who found them highly amusing.

Twain's first book, *The Celebrated Jumping Frog of Calaveras County and Other Sketches* (1867), was written in a well-established tradition of frontier humour – that is, full of grotesque episodes and tall tales. Significantly, in the preface the author is hailed as 'the Wild Humorist of the Pacific Slope', and therefore of a rather different breed from the mystic, intellectual authors, such as Emerson and Lowell, who dominated official culture.

In time, Twain imposed himself on America and gained acceptance as a great humorous writer. But the price – or so he believed – was a certain self-suppression. He accommodated himself to the genteel tradition and the puritanism of American society, allowing the standards of several respectable ladies (including his wife and daughters) to control his use of potentially 'vulgar' and 'indecorous' words.

He also concealed many of his unorthodox opinions. This may be why he wrote so little about American society in his own time, apart from the novel *The Gilded Age* (1873), in which Twain and his co-author, Charles Dudley Warner, launched a scathing attack on the contemporary financial and political corruption that so disgusted them.

He continued to state his views with such remarks as 'It could probably be shown with facts and figures that there is no distinctly native American criminal class except Congress'; but after *The Gilded Age*, Twain's major works centred on the past. He deals with the historic past in the burlesque *A Connecticut Yankee in King Arthur's Court*, and his own past in *The Adventures of Tom Sawyer* and *Huckleberry Finn*.

A river pilot
(above) Learning to navigate the Mississippi was a boyhood dream come true. Twain advanced from not knowing enough 'to pilot a cow down a lane', to becoming a skilled and respected river man. He also met the varied characters who people his books.

Quarry Farm
(left) The Twains' summer retreat, Quarry Farm, was situated on top of a high hill, 3 miles from Elmira, New York. Here Twain did most of his writing, notably Huckleberry Finn and Life on the Mississippi in the prodigious summer of 1883.

Tall tales
(right) Twain was first and foremost a storyteller. His 'Jumping Frog' story is a yarn told in the first person. It 'may be spun out to great length, and may wander round as much as it pleases, and arrive nowhere in particular.'

In these books, Twain's recoil from the present proved a creative boon, since his early years had an exceptionally strong hold on his memory and imagination. As he wrote *Tom Sawyer*, recollections flooded into his mind to surface in the story. And 'When the tank runs dry,' he discovered, 'you've only got to leave it alone and it will fill up again in time.' Though he had originally intended to end the book showing Tom as a disillusioned 40-year-old, Twain ultimately could not resist leaving it as a nostalgic, idealized picture of boyhood, 'a hymn, put into prose form to give it a worldly air'.

By contrast, Twain experienced great difficulties with *Huckleberry Finn*, which he began writing in 1876, soon after finishing *Tom Sawyer*. 'Began another boys' book – more to be at work than anything else. I have written 400 pages of it – therefore it is very nearly half done . . . I like it only tolerably well, as far as I have got, and may possibly pigeonhole it or burn the MS when it is done.'

In the event, Twain got stuck. He could not work out what to do with the runaways Huck and Jim, and he may well have been perplexed by the profound issues that were emerging in his 'boys' book'. He put it aside, took it up again a few years later, shelved it again, and only succeeded in completing it in 1884, stimulated by revisiting the South and writing *Life on the Mississippi* (1882). Twain's increasingly critical view of Southern society appears in *Huckleberry Finn* and reaches its climax in the novel *Pudd'nhead Wilson* (1894), which is also set in a town modelled on Hannibal, where he grew up.

'*I shall like it*, whether anybody else does or not', wrote Mark Twain of *Huckleberry Finn*. The book was, by genteel standards, an outrage. Tom Sawyer was an acceptable figure –

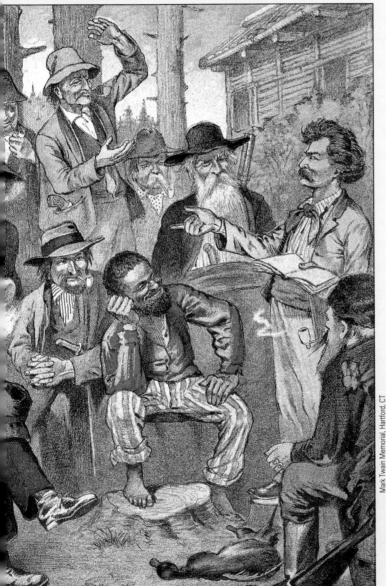

Don Quixote
(above) Cervantes, author of Don Quixote, was one of Twain's literary heroes. His lovable creation, the Man of La Mancha, tilted ineffectually at windmills and in so doing, as Twain believed, revealed the silliness of medieval – and Southern – chivalry.

William Dean Howells
(left) Novelist, critic and close friend of Twain, Howells published many of Twain's best pieces in his magazine, the Atlantic Monthly. Twain repaid his admiration, saying, 'You are really my only author, I wouldn't give a damn for the rest.'

The Writer at Work

Mary Evans Picture Library

F R I Interlaerner The Terrace at Posilion Naples/Fine Art Photographic Library

an endearing, good-hearted young scamp who would settle down in time; Huck, by contrast, was a ragged river-rat, a thieving, impenitent enemy of respectable society. Furthermore, Twain, the narrator of *Tom Sawyer*, had stepped aside and allowed Huck to tell his story in his own barbaric idiom.

The critics' reactions to the book proved that Twain's self-suppression was not caused by wholly imaginary fears. Despite his careful pruning of the text, *Huckleberry Finn* was widely attacked by literary critics, was excerpted in the *Century* magazine with numerous editorial changes, and was banned by the Concord Public Library as 'trash and suitable only for the slums'. Louisa May Alcott, famed writer of children's stories, stated trenchantly that 'If Mr Clemens cannot think of something better to tell our pure-minded lads and lasses, he had best stop writing for them.'

POPULAR TRIUMPH
Despite the critics, *Huckleberry Finn* proved to be Twain's biggest popular success. He capitalized on the fact, claiming that 'I have been misjudged from the very first. I have

never tried in even one single little instance to help cultivate the cultivated classes . . . I never had any ambition in that direction, but always hunted for bigger game – the masses.' In reality, he was deeply disturbed by his failure to win over the genteel establishment. It was almost five years before he published his next book, *A Connecticut Yankee in King Arthur's Court*, and that was intended to signal his 're-tirement from literature permanently' – an intention frustrated by the business disasters that bankrupted him.

Twain never again produced anything as 'offensive' as *Huckleberry Finn*, although his growing pessimism is reflected in published works such as *The Man That Corrupted Hadleyburg* (1900). But he piled up 'posthumous stuff', which was never meant to appear during his lifetime, including a mass of autobiographical musings and *The Mysterious Stranger*, a story full of cosmic gloom. In print he was prepared to take a political stance, attacking the rampant imperialism of the United States and the European powers, but he dared not publish *The War Prayer*, which savaged military glory and militant patriotism – 'I have told

the whole truth in that, and only dead men can tell the truth in this world.'

Twain habitually thrust the responsibility for his self-suppression on to his wife Livy. When she was ill, he wrote 'I have no editor – no censor.' But Livy was probably no more than the instrument of Twain's self-censorship. His desire for approval and acceptance was strong, and he basked unashamedly in the popularity of his last years, when he became America's Great Humorist.

'NOTHING SINCE'
Even after Twain's death, his very popularity concealed his achievement, although the publication of his 'posthumous stuff' revealed new sides to his genius. Only in recent decades has it been recognized that *Huckleberry Finn* is more than a marvellous boys' book – that it is a masterpiece in the native idiom. As Ernest Hemingway noted, 'all modern American literature comes from one book by Mark Twain called *Huckleberry Finn* . . . It's the best book we've had. All American writing comes from that. There was nothing before. There has been nothing as good since.'

20

The unknown sketch-writer Mark Twain leapt to prominence with *Jim Smiley and his Jumping Frog,* published on a larger scale as *The Celebrated Jumping Frog of Calaveras County* (1867). The travel sketches in *The Innocents Abroad* (1869) made him a household name; and in *Roughing It* (1872) and *Life on the Mississippi* (1883) he mixed travel and autobiography, embellishing them with comic exaggerations and an entertaining variety of improbable incidents.

In *The Adventures of Tom Sawyer* (1876) and *Huckleberry Finn* (1885), the novels on which Twain's fame mainly rests, Twain drew on boyhood memories to create classic, incisive portrayals of American life. His critical view of social and political life also lies behind the burlesque time-travel fantasy *A Connecticut Yankee in King Arthur's Court. Twain's* increasingly pessimistic view of life appears in his later fiction, notably the novel *Pudd'nhead Wilson* (1894) and the long story *The Man That Corrupted Hadleyburg* (1900) – powerful works that present a bleak view of humanity.

THE ADVENTURES OF TOM SAWYER

◆ 1876 ◆

The thoroughly believable friendship of Tom Sawyer and Huckleberry Finn (right) is central to this nostalgic novel of childhood (below). Huck figures as the disreputable friend of the hero, Tom Sawyer. Tom and his priggish, hypocritical brother Sid live with their good-hearted Aunt Polly in St Petersburg, on the Mississippi. Tom is an endearing scapegrace, always in and out of trouble for playing hookey, telling extravagantly tall tales, and acting out his fantasies as the leader of robber gangs. He is also highly resourceful, and one of the most famous scenes in the book occurs when Tom is condemned to whitewash a fence as punishment (right). He convinces several other boys that this is a thoroughly enjoyable task, and they actually pay him for the privilege of taking over his chore. The main action begins when Tom and Huck go to a graveyard at midnight and see a half-breed, Injun Joe, stab the town doctor and place the knife in the hand of his drunken companion, Muff Potter. Tom must try to prevent a terrible miscarriage of justice – there may even be money in it for him and Huck.

After the grander, more ambitious and greatly acclaimed sequel, *Huckleberry Finn* (1885), Mark Twain wrote two more books about the boys, *Tom Sawyer Abroad* (1894) and *Tom Sawyer, Detective* (1896), and contemplated a reunion story in which the two met in old age and died within the book.

W. Homer: Snap the Whip, Metropolitan Museum of Art, Gift of Christian A. Zabriskie

PUDD'NHEAD WILSON

◆ 1894 ◆

Roxy, a pale mulatto slave (left) in the household of Percy Driscoll is given charge of her owner's baby son, Tom, since she is already suckling a baby boy born to her on the same day. Fearful that her own slave–child will be 'sold down the river', Roxy switches the babies so that her boy, Chambers, will grow up as 'Marse Tom Driscoll'. But 'Tom', utterly spoiled by the Driscolls, turns out a worthless spendthrift and a thief. Eventually he murders his guardian, Judge Driscoll, while in the act of robbing him. Suspicion falls on a pair of twins, and only the lawyer Pudd'nhead Wilson knows enough to rectify the fatal mistake. Small-town Dawson's Landing can make no sense of Wilson – he is too clever, eccentric and advanced for their comprehension. But he alone is able ultimately to unravel the tangled identities of the book's two main characters.

This is much darker than Twain's previous Mississippi novels, written when he was in a state of depression, and deeply disillusioned with American society.

J.J. Eastman: Old Kentucky Home, Life in the South. (Detail) New York Historical Society/Bridgeman Art Library

Loading Cotton on the Mississippi, Currier and Ives, American Museum in Britain, Bath/Bridgeman Art Library

LIFE ON THE MISSISSIPPI

◆ 1883 ◆

The great age of the steamboat (above), before the American Civil War, is recalled by Twain in a mixture of history, travel narrative and personal reminiscence. The first half of the book consists of a series of articles originally published in the *Atlantic Monthly* magazine in 1875. They capture the glamour of the ships which every boy along the river dreamed of joining, and the activity unleashed by the cry, "S-t-e-a-m-boat a-comin". Twain also describes his own training as a steamboat pilot, "the only unfettered and entirely independent human being".

The second half of *Life on the Mississippi* was written seven years after the magazine articles, and was inspired by a riverboat trip from St Louis to New Orleans. Twain now finds the great age nothing but a memory; the railway has vanquished the steamboat, the river has changed beyond recognition, and he himself has fallen out of love with the South. Chapter Three contains an episode originally intended for *Huckleberry Finn*, and there are many links between the two books, both of which draw on Twain's return visit to the once-enthralling scenes of his youth.

THE MAN THAT CORRUPTED HADLEYBURG

◆ 1900 ◆

Hadleyburg is a smugly self-satisfied community (above) proud of its reputation as "the most honest and upright town in all the region round about". Then a mysterious stranger launches a clever scheme to discredit it, tempting 19 of its most respected citizens with the prospect of $40,000 in gold. Everyone falls for the hoax and Hadleyburg is exposed as a town of hypocrites, liars and cheats. Only one man in the town wins an undeserved reputation for being uniquely incorruptible. Ultimately, the citizens realize that there is just one thing they can do to restore the utterly tarnished name of Hadleyburg . . .

This is widely regarded as the best story published by Twain in the last, increasingly pessimistic phase of his career. One critic claims it as proof that Twain was 'more than a humorist, that he was, in fact, a great teacher, moralist, philosopher – the greatest . . . of his age'.

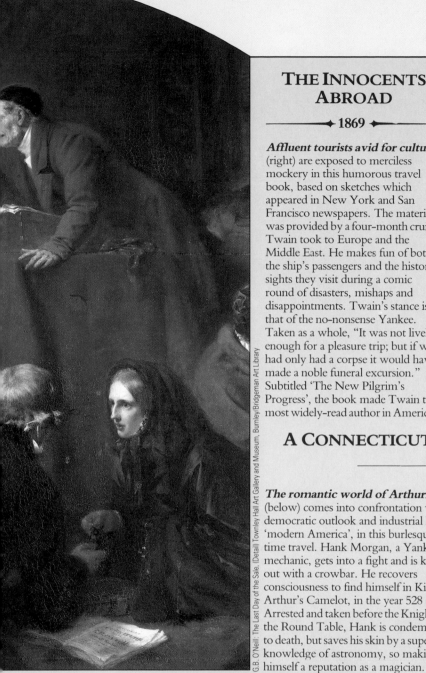

THE INNOCENTS ABROAD

◆ 1869 ◆

Affluent tourists avid for culture (right) are exposed to merciless mockery in this humorous travel book, based on sketches which appeared in New York and San Francisco newspapers. The material was provided by a four-month cruise Twain took to Europe and the Middle East. He makes fun of both the ship's passengers and the historic sights they visit during a comic round of disasters, mishaps and disappointments. Twain's stance is that of the no-nonsense Yankee. Taken as a whole, "It was not lively enough for a pleasure trip; but if we had only had a corpse it would have made a noble funeral excursion." Subtitled 'The New Pilgrim's Progress', the book made Twain the most widely-read author in America.

K. Spitweg: The English in the Country, National Gallery, Berlin/Archiv für Kunst und Geschichte

A CONNECTICUT YANKEE IN KING ARTHUR'S COURT

◆ 1889 ◆

The romantic world of Arthurian legend (below) comes into confrontation with the democratic outlook and industrial know-how of 'modern America', in this burlesque novel of time travel. Hank Morgan, a Yankee mechanic, gets into a fight and is knocked out with a crowbar. He recovers consciousness to find himself in King Arthur's Camelot, in the year 528 (right). Arrested and taken before the Knights of the Round Table, Hank is condemned to death, but saves his skin by a superior knowledge of astronomy, so making himself a reputation as a magician.

Having brought electricity and other technological benefits to sixth-century Britain, he goes to the aid of the common people. But now nobility and church unite against him.

G.B. O'Neill: The Last Day of the Sale, (Detail) Townley Hall Art Gallery and Museum, Burnley/Bridgeman Art Library

C. Dixon: The Potato Pickers, Roy Miles Fine Paintings/Bridgeman Art Library

The Mississippi was more than a river to Mark Twain – it showed him the world, and inspired his life and his art. The captions are quoted from his works.

The vivid characters who enliven the pages of *The Adventures of Huckleberry Finn* are no more memorably drawn by the author than is the mighty Mississippi itself. Mark Twain was enthralled by the 'Father of Waters', as the native Ojibwa Indians described the great river. He spent his childhood on the banks of the Mississippi, fulfilled a dream by becoming a riverboat pilot and throughout his career as a celebrated author and raconteur drew endlessly on a store of river wit and wisdom. Just as early Victorian London is universally viewed through the eyes of Charles Dickens, so the Mississippi of the years preceding the American Civil War is etched in our imagination by the pen of Mark Twain.

A glance at a map of the North American continent shows clearly enough why the Mississippi loomed so large in the development of the young United States. Together with its great tributaries, the Ohio joining it from the north-east, and the Missouri from the north-west, the Mississippi drains a vast area – water from 31 states and two Canadian provinces. The entire river system covers an extent of 1900 miles (north to south)

by 1400 miles (east to west), making the Mississippi basin about ten times the size of the British Isles.

The river forms a natural divide between the eastern and western United States. As settlers moved westward during the early years of the 19th century, prime locations on the Mississippi served as stepping stones to the deep interior of the continent. The most important of these was St Louis, Missouri, situated on the west bank of the Mississippi 100 miles south of Twain's childhood home in Hannibal. Originally an 18th-century French trading post, St Louis was, by the 1830s, a flourishing city at the crossroads of westward expansion, yet only a generation away from the raw realities of frontier life.

The Mississippi meanwhile was assuming a much greater importance as a commercial route linking the rural west and north-west with the large urban centres along the Atlantic seaboard. Canals and railroads would in time transform east-west communications, but during the first half of the 19th century the Mississippi River provided the vital connection between these regions.

A Midnight Race on the Mississippi: Currier and Ives/Peter Newark's Western Americana

New Orleans docklands
(below left) "It was always the custom for the boats to leave New Orleans between four and five o'clock in the afternoon. From three o'clock onward they would be burning rosin and pitch pine . . . and so had the picturesque spectacle of a rank, some two or three miles long of tall, ascending columns of coal-black smoke, a colonnade . . ."

The Levee-New Orleans: Currier and Ives/Peter Newark's Western Americana

Mary Evans Picture Library

The Mississippi provided him with a unique view which was to remain with him throughout a long and varied life: "When I find a well-drawn character in fiction or biography, I generally take a warm personal interest in him, for the reason that I have known him before – met him on the river."

This may seem a tall claim, but the Mississippi did indeed contain varied representatives of the human race. By 1835, the year of Twain's birth, the steam tonnage on the river was nearly half that of the British Empire. And it multiplied six fold during the next 15 years, by which time more than a thousand steamboats regularly plied its waters. New York was firmly established as America's leading Atlantic port, yet in 1843 New Orleans handled twice its marine tonnage.

THE HUMAN SPECTRUM

Activity on this sort of scale was bound to attract a motley crowd of humanity: thieves, whores, confidence tricksters, sailors, merchants and the whole spectrum of folk found in hustling, bustling ports anywhere in the world. Slaves were also a common sight, for the institution of negro slavery still existed along part of the river's course. Twain hated slavery – having observed it at close quarters in his youth, in the slave state of Missouri. Illinois, on the opposite bank, was a free state (that is, slave-free) – which was why Huck's companion, the slave Jim, could float south on a raft and still hope to make good his bid for freedom.

A whole range of characters was caught up in the web of slavery besides the slaves themselves. There were slave owners (some humane, many vicious); slave traders, to whom the slaves were simply a commodity; pitiless slave catchers in pursuit of runaways like Jim; and the assembled crowd of bidders and onlookers attending slave auctions, where fearful slaves faced the dreaded prospect of being 'sold down the river' – to toil in the cotton fields of the Deep South.

A unique class, not directly involved in slavery but largely created by its existence, was the 'poor white trash', of whom Huck's drunken father is an unlovely

Night work
(above) "Here was something fresh – this thing of getting up in the middle of the night to go to work . . . I knew that boats ran all night, but somehow I had never happened to reflect that somebody had to get out of a warm bed to run them. I began to fear that piloting was not quite so romantic as I had imagined it was . . ."

As a child growing up in Hannibal, Twain watched fascinated as an endless stream of river traffic carried supplies and manufactured goods up river to interior towns and beyond to the western hinterland; while the agricultural and natural wealth of the interior was transported down river to the vibrant, wealthy port of New Orleans.

The young Twain also observed a welter of assorted humanity. In *Life on the Mississippi*, he says of his days as a river pilot that it equipped him with a telescoped education in the ways of the world. This life on the river allowed him to become "personally and familiarly acquainted with all the different types of human nature that are to be found in fiction, biography or history".

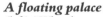

A floating palace
(left) "When he stepped aboard a fine steamboat, he entered a new and marvellous world . . . big chandeliers every little way, each an April shower of glittering glass drops."

Rafts on the river
(right) "Pilots bore a mortal hatred to these craft . . . All of a sudden, on a murky night . . . an agonized voice . . . would wail out: 'Whar'n the —— you goin' to! Cain't you see nothin', you dash-dashed aig-suckin', sheep-stealin', one-eyed son of a stuffed monkey!'"

Human trade

(above and left) "At first my father owned slaves but by and by he sold them and hired others by the year from the farmers. For a girl of fifteen he paid twenty dollars a year . . . and for an able-bodied man he paid from seventy-five to a hundred dollars a year and gave him two suits of jeans and two pairs of "stogy" shoes – an outfit that cost about three dollars." "I vividly remember seeing a dozen black men and women chained to one another, once, and lying in a group on the pavement, awaiting shipment to the Southern slave market. Those were the saddest faces I have ever seen." Twain was never to forget such sights as these.

example. Because slaves performed so many tasks associated in 'free' societies with the lower orders – agricultural labour, domestic service and miscellaneous menial jobs – the American South spawned a class of such social drop-outs.

These poor whites had neither land nor slaves, nor a handle on respectable employment, and they were left to shift for themselves in a society never noted for its charity to 'losers'. In this sorry condition they were prey to the usual vices that are associated with permanent demoralization – drunkenness, idleness, petty criminality and debauchery. As they loitered around the river landing they could take pathetic solace from the fact that they were a cut above the despised black slaves, who had not even a toe-hold on the lowest rung of the social ladder.

The river landings were by times sleepy and frenetic, as the riverboats bore down on them to discharge passengers and goods, and to take aboard produce and supplies, most critically firewood, which they consumed voraciously. The wood pile by the landing, indeed, was a permanent feature, and the hapless runaway slaves sometimes found a convenient hiding-place in it. Most slaves around the landings were, of course, not runaways, but roustabouts who loaded and unloaded the boats. Their doleful chants and songs were pleasing enough to white ears, although some of the lyrics on occasion might have raised a few qualms:

'We raise de wheat,
Dey gib us de corn;
We bake de bread,
Dey gib us de cruss;
We peel de meat,
Dey gib us de skin;
And dat's de way
Dey takes us in.'

MISSISSIPPI STEAMBOATS

In reality, as much as in folklore, the dominant image of the Mississippi during its halcyon days was the steamboat. Their boastful description as 'floating palaces' was little exaggeration. They were as opulent as quick profits could make them, as fast as the steam-powered paddle-wheels could drive them, and as shallow-bottomed as ingenuity could contrive.

The muddy Mississippi was – and is – a treacherous river to navigate, with hidden snags everywhere, for the swirling currents deposit a sandbar today where there was a safe channel yesterday. Wags said that the boats needed so little water that they could have floated as easily on the volume of whisky consumed during the journey.

There were two types: stern-wheelers and the more glamorous side-wheelers, which came to dominate the trade during its peak years (the 1850s). These were splendid creations, with ornate exterior pillars and balustrades in sparkling paintwork, gleaming brass fittings and proud tall smoke-stacks. Crowning this 'wedding-cake' edifice was a glass-sided wheelhouse, which was the pilot's domain. By night the paddle-wheelers were even more spectacular. 'Like moving mountains of light and flame, so brilliantly are these enormous

Abolitionist author

(above) Harriet Beecher Stowe's book, Uncle Tom's Cabin, was an electrifying indictment of slavery, which had a crucial effect on the climate of public opinion. She lived near Twain who met her on at least one occasion and pronounced it "a very gay time".

E. Degas: New Orleans, Cotton Exchange. Musée des Beaux Arts. Pau/Bridgeman Art Library

The profits of cotton

(right) "A cotton-planter's estimate of the average margin of profit on planting, in his section: One man and mule will raise ten acres of cotton, worth, say, $500; cost of producing, say $350; net profit, $150, or $15 per acre. There is also a profit now from the cottonseed, which formerly had little value – none where much transportation was necessary. In sixteen hundred pounds crude cotton, four hundred are lint, worth, say, ten cents a pound; and twelve hundred pounds of seed, worth $12 or $13 per ton. Maybe in future even the stems will not be thrown away. Mr Edward Atkinson says that for each bale of cotton there are fifteen hundred pounds of stems, and that these are very rich in phospate of lime of potash . . ."

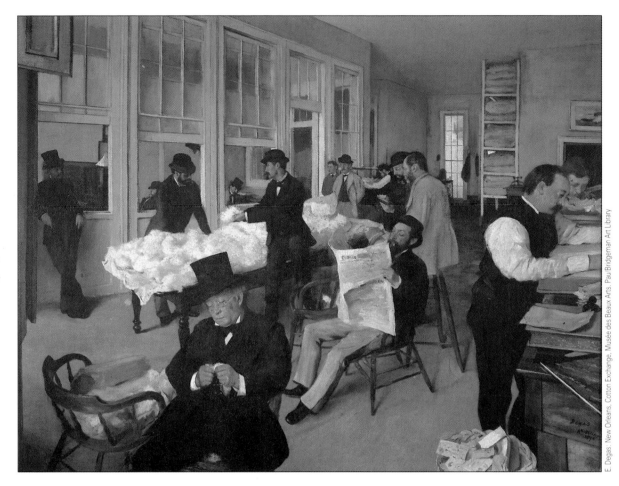

Planter's Home/Peter Newark's Western Americana

Temples of slavery

(above) "Every town . . . along that vast stretch of . . . river . . . had a best dwelling . . . large grassy yard, with paling fence painted white . . . square, two-storey 'frame' house, painted white and porticoed like a Grecian temple . . . fluted columns and Corinthian capitals . . ."

gers also enjoyed the luxury of elegantly appointed private cabins, which ran along both sides of the main deck. One captain had the novel idea of naming each cabin after a State of the Union, thus giving us the word 'stateroom'.

The passengers were an exotic mix of immigrants and merchants, fur traders and cotton planters, slaves and grandees, ladies and ladies-of-easy-virtue, cutthroats, confidence tricksters and scoundrels of every rank from the raffish to the riff-raffish. Casting calculating glances over this motley mix were the professional gamblers, easily enough identified by their ingratiating manners and elegant attire. Marathon card games could last the entire journey, with real fortunes at stake. It was not unheard of for $25,000 to turn on a single card, and when a plantation owner was down on his luck he could always stake his slaves, and if worst came to worst the plantation itself.

Among these indulgences lurked constant hazards. One mistake by the pilot could lead to disaster. Fire was an even greater danger, packed as these flimsy wooden craft often were with bales of cotton. An exploding boiler, a shower of sparks from the smoke-stacks, a carelessly tossed cigar, and flames could engulf the crowded boat with appalling loss of life. Steamboat disasters claimed thousands of lives during these years, and the evocative phrase 'floating palaces' had an ominous twin – 'swimming volcanoes'.

To such accidental hazards were sometimes added ones of a more deliberate nature. The display of affluence was a lure for river pirates. They might come

leviathans illuminated outside and inside', one English lady traveller wrote. It was not uncommon to see steamboats engaged in a midnight race. Spirits ran high, on-board and off, as onlookers cheered their favourites on from crowded shores.

The boats' interiors could fairly be described as palatial, with panelled walls, filigree woodwork, inlaid floors, stained-glass skylights, paintings, chandeliers and mirrors. Imported French chefs provided first-class passengers with sumptuous fare and fine wines, with the best linen, china and silverware. First-class passen-

Federal Troops Entering a Southern Mansion, The Corcoran Gallery of Art/Weidenfeld Archive

H. Bonham: Nearing the Issue at the Cockpit/The Corcoran Gallery of Art

The end of an era

(above) "In the South, the war is what A.D. is elsewhere; they date from it. All day long you hear things 'placed' as having happened since the waw; or du'in the waw; or befo' the waw . . . every individual was visited . . . by that tremendous episode."

Faces of the South

(below) "We went to a cockpit in New Orleans . . . There were men and boys there of all ages and all colors, and of many languages and nationalities. But I noticed one quite conspicuous and surprising absence: the traditional brutal faces."

aboard as passengers and wait for an appropriate moment to strike, robbing the wealthy at gunpoint; or they might storm the boat from the shore, when it put in at a landing for fuel.

Life on a Mississippi steamboat was not to everyone's taste, and fastidious Europeans who experienced it were sometimes unimpressed by the behaviour of their American cousins. Anthony Trollope's mother, Frances, caused a furore in the United States in the early 1830s, when she published *Domestic Manners of the Americans*, a somewhat jaundiced account of her lengthy travels there a few years before.

She liked little of what she saw, and when it came to the masculine company aboard a steamboat, she was downright scathing. Tobacco chewing was ubiquitous, and Mrs Trollope was utterly revolted by 'the incessant, remorseless spitting of Americans'. She describes the saloon as being well-appointed and well-carpeted: 'But oh! That carpet! I will not, I may not describe its condition; indeed it requires the pen of a Swift to do it justice. Let no one who wishes to receive agreeable impressions of American manners, commence their travels in a Mississippi steamboat; for myself, it is with all sincerity I declare, that I would infinitely prefer sharing the apartment of a party of well conditioned pigs to being confined to its cabin.'

Huck Finn's creator thought Mrs Trollope entitled to her opinion, but his observing eye was usually not directed towards the floor. In his descriptions of his Mississippi travels, "there was things which he stretched, but mainly he told the truth."

F. SCOTT FITZGERALD

◆ *1896-1940* ◆

No writer has more closely personified the glamour and
heartbreak of the American dream than F. Scott Fitzgerald. As
a young writer he evoked the affluent, optimistic Jazz Age of
1920s America; later, the decline of his marriage, his wife's
breakdown and his own slide into drunkenness found an echo
in the Depression. But Fitzgerald's stories and novels are more
than chronicles – they represent 'the history of all aspiration
– not just the American dream but the human dream'.

BEAUTIFUL AND DAMNED

Fitzgerald set out to be one of the greatest writers who ever lived. But in staking his all on a grand, illusory lifestyle, he lost both talent and life prematurely.

Scott Fitzgerald's meteoric rise to fame and riches sowed the seeds of a tragic, drink-sodden decline. His doomed marriage and the struggle he put up in later years to redeem his reputation are aptly summed up in his own words: 'Show me a hero and I will write you a tragedy.'

Francis Scott Key Fitzgerald was born on 24 September 1896 in St Paul, Minnesota, and named after an ancestor on his father's side who wrote the words of the American national anthem, 'The Star Spangled Banner'. His mother Mollie's parents were Irish immigrants, while his father, who had helped the Confederate cause during the American Civil War, was of old Southern stock. This clash of blood, said Fitzgerald, instilled in him 'a two cylinder inferiority complex' that made him acutely aware of his own modest beginnings – at the age of nine he convinced himself that he was really a royal foundling, 'a son of a king, a king who ruled the whole world'. In fact, his father,

Edward Fitzgerald, was a failed businessman who scraped a living selling groceries.

Fitzgerald was a rather precocious and vain schoolboy. At St Paul Academy, and later at a Catholic boarding school in Hackensack, New Jersey, he gained a reputation as a show-off – indeed, he never lost this need to be the centre of attention. He turned to writing as a way of courting popularity, by his own account becoming 'an inveterate author and a successful, not to say brilliant debater and writer'.

A PRIVILEGED EDUCATION

In 1913 he went to Princeton, the Ivy League university he eulogized in *This Side of Paradise* – 'the pleasantest country club in America', he called it. Princeton's intimidating social hierarchies and systems of protocol strengthened Fitzgerald's sense of destiny – 'If I couldn't be perfect I wouldn't be anything', he confided to his diary – and he set

Princeton University Library

Prophecy
Scott's mother (left) recalled him asking, 'when I get to be a big boy can I have all the things I oughtn't . . . ?'

Adored son
Months before Scott was born, his parents lost their first two children. Inevitably their surviving son was spoiled. His father, Edward (shown with him, left), failed in business, then was dismissed ignominiously. However, the family had a generous inheritance on which they could depend.

Sense of belonging
Famous and footloose, Scott still chose to see his own child born in his native St Paul, Minnesota (below).

Hamm Building and St. Peter S

Shelron Collectors' Shop

great store by belonging to the most exclusive dining club and cultivating the most advantageous friendships.

John Peale Bishop was the first friend to share his commitment to writing, and under his influence Fitzgerald began to take himself seriously as a writer. He wrote for the campus magazines the *Princeton Tiger* and the *Lit*, edited by poet and critic Edmund Wilson, and caused a stir with his lyrics for a Princeton musical that went on a national tour. His writing achievements were beginning to earn him the sort of celebrity he craved, but in 1916 his continuing academic failure cost him the presidency of the Princeton theatrical Triangle Club, a setback he never forgot – 'There were to be no badges of pride, no medals, after all', he wrote more than 20 years later.

A REFUGE FROM FAILURE

When the time came to leave Princeton, Fitzgerald knew beyond doubt where his future lay – 'I want to be one of the greatest writers who ever lived', he told an astonished Edmund Wilson. His immediate future was decided by the United States' entry into World War I. He joined the army as a second lieutenant in October 1917 and began writing a novel called 'The Romantic Egotist' (later developed into *This Side of Paradise*). Among the local girls who dated the soldiers from his army camp near Montgomery, Alabama, was a high-spirited 18-year-old called Zelda Sayre. Soon she and Fitzgerald had fallen in love.

Patti McConville/Image Bank

Student aspirations
Princeton (above) meant sport, glamour, notoriety, clubs, writing and status. Scott rejoiced in all but studying.

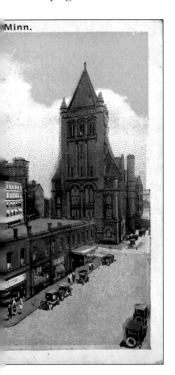

Key Dates

1896 born St Paul, Minnesota

1913 attends Princeton University

1918 meets Zelda Sayre

1920 *This Side of Paradise*. Marries Zelda

1921 birth of daughter Scottie

1924 returns to France

1925 *The Great Gatsby*. Meets Hemingway

1930 Zelda's first breakdown

1932 Zelda's second breakdown

1934 Zelda's third breakdown. *Tender Is the Night*

1936 'The Crack-Up'

1937 works in Hollywood

1940 dies in Hollywood

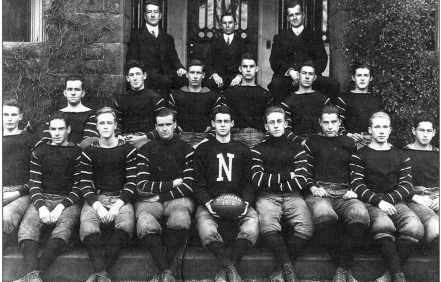

Princeton University Library

Hero of the field
Fitzgerald's footballing prowess at Newman School (above) paled on the Princeton field. So instead of becoming a football star, he decided to win fame and fortune by means of his pen.

They seemed a perfectly matched couple. An aspiring dancer, Zelda was beautiful and wilful and sought the same things in life as Fitzgerald – success, glamour and, above all, fame. Accordingly Fitzgerald went to New York after being discharged from the army and tried to establish himself as a writer. But the walls of his room were soon papered with rejection slips, and when Zelda called off their proposed marriage, the despairing

Lloyd Arnold/John F Kennedy Library

Fitzgerald sought solace in drink. Increasingly alcohol would become a refuge from failure.

He went back to St Paul to work on a new novel, in the hope that literary success would bring Zelda round, and in September 1919 *This Side of Paradise* was accepted by Scribners' editor Maxwell Perkins. This marked the start of a unique, lifelong friendship and collaboration between author and editor.

Back in New York, Fitzgerald began to sell his short stories to the *Saturday Evening Post* – the popular magazine market would prove his steadiest source of income – and set about enjoy-

'The real thing'
Three years younger than Fitzgerald, his friend Ernest Hemingway (left) had a breadth of experience and vigour which Scott admired and envied.

Riviera life
A stylish, indulgent life was relatively cheap on the Riviera (right) for Americans. When money ran short, Fitzgerald said, 'I can't reduce our scale of living.'

ing the fruits of early success, spending extravagantly and giving recklessly big tips. His attitude to money was coloured by his modest origins. 'I have never been able to forgive the rich for being rich', he wrote. As if to prove a point, he squandered the high fees he commanded for his stories and other writings, and lived for much of his life in the shadow of debt, relying on advances from Max Perkins and his agent, Harold Ober.

This Side of Paradise was published in March 1920 to great critical acclaim. The next month Fitzgerald and Zelda were married in New York. None were more closely identified with the era of extravagant living, in all its exuberance and excess, than Scott and Zelda Fitzgerald.

NEVER HAPPY AGAIN
At 23, Fitzgerald was rich and famous. He rode on the roofs of taxi cabs and jumped into fountains, gave endless newspaper interviews and got drunk at countless parties – 'I had everything I wanted and knew I would never be happy again', he said. But the seeds of later failure and despair were already being sown. His drinking had started to get out of hand and Zelda began to resent his success and the attention it brought him. They

Post-War euphoria
The celebration of peace (below) began a decade-long party in which Scott and Zelda joined with a kind of desperate determination.

George Luks: Armistice Night 1918/Collection of Whitney Museum of American Art/Anonymous gift

ZELDA

A talented dancer, painter and author, Zelda Fitzgerald was not content to live in the shadow of her husband. The letters they exchanged express pain and resentment – but keen, enduring love, too. After Scott's death, she lived quietly with her mother, returning to hospital during fits of depression. During one such visit, in 1948, Zelda was one of nine patients who died in a fire. She was buried alongside Scott.

quarrelled and made up frequently – a pattern that increased and intensified over the years.

In the spring of 1921 they made their first trip to Europe, shortly after Fitzgerald had been beaten up by a bouncer in a New York speakeasy when Zelda had egged him on to start a fight. They stayed in London, where they met Lady Randolph and Winston Churchill, and visited Paris, Venice, Florence and Rome. On their return in the summer they lived in St Paul. Their daughter Scottie was born in October as Fitzgerald worked on his second novel.

The Beautiful and Damned received a disappointing reception when it came out in March 1922. Later that year the Fitzgeralds rented a house at Great Neck on Long Island and became friendly with the writer Ring Lardner, who lived nearby. 'Mr Fitzgerald is a novelist and Mrs Fitzgerald a novelty' was Lardner's witty description of the celebrated couple. The rounds of parties and glittering social functions on Long Island are reflected in Fitzgerald's third novel, *The Great Gatsby*. But it was an expensive way of life. In 1923 Fitzgerald earned almost 30,000 dollars, yet had practically nothing to show for it by the year's end.

They returned to France in the spring of 1924, renting a villa on the Riviera near St Raphaël. Zelda's brief affair with a French airman threatened their marriage, and though they patched things up, Fitzgerald had been badly shaken – 'I knew something had happened which could never be repaired', he said. They moved to

Paris in 1925, when *The Great Gatsby* was published to respectful reviews but indifferent sales.

Fitzgerald had already alerted Scribners to a talented but struggling young American writer living in Paris called Ernest Hemingway – 'He's the real thing', Fitzgerald told Max Perkins. He now made Hemingway's acquaintance, and from the first their friendship was marked by a sense of awe and deference on Fitzgerald's part, despite the fact that he was the more established writer.

Paris in 1925 was an exhilarating place, at once a haven and a magnet for the most brilliant artistic talents of the decade. The Fitzgeralds lived its life to the full, spending riotous evenings in the cabarets of Montmartre and the Left Bank haunts of artists and intellectuals.

OVER THE EDGE

They spent 1926 back on the Riviera, where the favourable exchange rate made living cheap for Americans. Fitzgerald's drinking was now getting worse. He would introduce himself by declaring, 'I'm an alcoholic', and his craving for attention made him behave abominably when drunk: at one dinner party he threw fruit at a guest, attacked a friend, and smashed glasses. Zelda's behaviour, too, was becoming erratic and dangerous. She and Fitzgerald regularly goaded each other into acts of drunken bravado, on one occasion diving into the sea from a clifftop. Returning to America at the end of the year, he summed up the year 1926 frankly – 'Futile, shameful useless . . . Self disgust. Health gone'.

Their marriage was now in serious trouble, in the grip of a vicious circle of resentment and retaliation made worse by Fitzgerald's constant drinking. On his first excursion to Hollywood at the beginning of 1927 – to write a flapper comedy that was never made – he met and fell for a young actress called Lois Moran. Outraged and hurt by their association, Zelda started a fire in their hotel

The Keystone Collection

A troubled childhood
The Fitzgeralds' only child, Frances ('Scottie'), had a disrupted, unstable childhood. (The family is pictured above setting sail yet again for Europe.) When she grew up flighty and headstrong, Fitzgerald was a fiercely strict and critical father.

bathroom and, on their trip back to New York, threw her watch, an expensive gift from Fitzgerald, from the train window.

In an attempt to reform his dissolute lifestyle and get down to some serious work on his next novel, Fitzgerald rented a secluded mansion called Ellerslie on the Delaware River. But the bright lights of New York proved too much of a temptation and he and Zelda made regular trips there – 'We come up for a weekend', wrote Zelda, 'then wake up and it's Thursday.'

They returned to Paris in 1928. Zelda, who had resumed her ballet training two years before, now became obsessed with her ambition to make the grade as a top-flight ballerina. Unable to work properly himself, Fitzgerald resented her discipline and was angered when she was too tired to go drinking with him. He went on solo drinking sprees instead, and twice ended up in jail.

The Wall Street Crash of 1929, which signalled the end of the boom era, must have struck an ominous note with Scott and Zelda Fitzgerald. They had just returned to Paris from another summer on the Riviera – Zelda's mental health was deteriorating rapidly and on the drive north she had grabbed the steering wheel and tried to steer the car over a cliff. In the spring of the following year, after several suicide attempts, she was admitted to a Swiss clinic where she was diagnosed as a schizophrenic.

Fitzgerald visited her often and they exchanged many soul-searching letters, in one of which he blamed her breakdown on 'your almost megalomaniacal selfishness and my insane indulgence to drink'. He came to the sad conclusion that 'We ruined ourselves.'

Zelda made progress during 1931 and in

Wide World Photos

Fact or Fiction

THE ORIGINAL GATSBY

Jay Gatsby was partly based on a Long Island neighbour of the Fitzgeralds, Max Gerlach – 'said to be General Pershing's nephew . . . in trouble over bootlegging'. In the family scrapbook Gerlach used that favourite Gatsby catchphrase 'old sport'.

Gatsby's chilling partner in crime, Meyer Wolfsheim, who "fixed the World Series back in 1919", was modelled on the well-known gambler Arnold Rothstein (right), whom Fitzgerald had met.

and shameful. The *New York Post* described him as a drunk with the 'pitiful expression of a cruelly beaten child'.

Fitzgerald's debts stood at 40,000 dollars, and he was at a particularly low ebb, when in June 1937 MGM hired him as a scriptwriter at a salary of 1,000 dollars a week, a move that resurrected his life and career. He went to Hollywood with renewed optimism and a determination not to drink. Although his 18 months at the studio yielded just one screen credit, as co-writer of *Three Comrades* starring Robert Taylor and Margaret Sullavan, he was not the washed-up failure he has sometimes been painted.

THE LAST BATTLE

He was to be with Zelda just once more, on a drunken trip to Cuba in 1939. By this time MGM had failed to renew his contract and his self-discipline had disintegrated. His girlfriend, Sheilah Graham – an English gossip columnist working in Hollywood – put up with his drunken rages and even forgave him for threatening her with a revolver. She and Max Perkins stood by him to the last as he battled against sickness and disillusion to complete *The Last Tycoon*, the novel that he hoped would re-establish him as the greatest American writer of his generation.

At the end of November 1940 Fitzgerald suffered a heart attack in a drugstore on Sunset Boulevard, and moved to Sheilah Graham's apartment to convalesce. It was there, on 21 December 1940, that he collapsed with a second heart attack, and died shortly afterwards, at the age of 44. *The Last Tycoon* remained unfinished. Scott Fitzgerald provided his own, cruelly fitting epitaph – 'Then I was drunk for many years, and then I died'.

September she was discharged from the clinic. Fitzgerald's summary of the year was optimistic – 'From darkness to light'. Back in the United States, they settled in Zelda's home town of Montgomery, where she began a novel that was eventually published as *Save Me the Waltz*. But the strain of hard work proved too much, and in February 1932 Zelda was admitted to a psychiatric clinic in Baltimore. Fitzgerald rented a 15-room house nearby and began to count the cost of his own deteriorating health. In the next four years he would be admitted to hospital nine times, for alcoholism and for tuberculosis. Meanwhile he started his final assault on the novel that was to become *Tender is the Night*.

The novel was published in April 1934. The following month Zelda's condition became catatonic, and Fitzgerald had to face the fact that she would never get better – 'I left my capacity for hoping on the little roads that led to Zelda's sanitarium', he wrote. In despair over Zelda, and disappointed by the lukewarm reception of *Tender is the Night*, Fitzgerald spent much of the summer of 1934 drunk, writing his wife sad letters full of wistful reminiscences of 'The good things, and the first years together'.

By now Fitzgerald was a sick, tired and depressed man of 38 whose writing skills were on the wane. The days were over when he could produce highly paid magazine stories to order, and money was a constant worry. In 1936 *Esquire* magazine published a series of confessional essays known as 'The Crack-Up' in which Fitzgerald analysed the loss of his creative powers and the sadness and waste of his life. His candour alienated his public and embarrassed close friends – including Hemingway, who thought the essays cowardly

The Kobal Collection

Hollywood hacking
The late 1930s was a Golden Age of Hollywood escapist entertainment (above). For 18 months, Fitzgerald worked for MGM. He earned more money than ever before, but the work was thankless, second-rate hack writing. (His work on Gone with the Wind *was not even credited.) And he got nothing else written. He no longer lived recklessly, for he was under the good influence of Sheilah Graham – a resilient, unselfish woman who tolerated his drinking and tried to dry him out. The two are pictured right on a trip to Mexico. But the puritanical Scott felt guilt about the extra-marital relationship, exhibiting this in recriminations and drunken rows. Sheilah did not ask him to marry her, but did want a child; he was outraged.*

THE GREAT GATSBY

In the dogged pursuit of his one, impossibly romantic dream, Gatsby sinks into a vortex of meaningless dazzle and casual violence.

*T*he Great Gatsby is an immensely powerful novel that has achieved a mythical quality for its dramatic evocation of an impossible dream of love. The tragic consequences of that dream are embodied in the life of Gatsby, who finds that all the riches of the world cannot restore his lost love. The characters move slowly through the long hot summer of 1922, drinking, dancing and searching for something to ease the boredom of their empty lives. Fitzgerald's classic novel is both a fascinating social document of the 1920s and a timeless love story.

GUIDE TO THE PLOT

Nick Carraway, the young narrator of the story, arrives in New York City and rents a house for the summer in West Egg, the unfashionable side of the Long Island peninsula. He finds himself neighbour to Jay Gatsby, the mysterious millionaire whose lavish parties are attended by crowds of people, none of whom seem to know their host.

Nick is invited to dinner by his wealthy cousin Daisy, who lives with her arrogant, boorish husband, Tom Buchanan, across the bay in fashionable East Egg.

"He did extraordinarily well in the war"
(below) Gatsby's uniform gave him access to Daisy and her enviable world. But he delayed too long in returning.

Mary Evans Picture Library

Hopelessly romantic
(above) Gatsby and Daisy dance to the music of a "tuning-fork . . . struck upon a star".

Jordan Baker, their other guest that night, tells Nick that Tom is having an affair.

Disturbed by the cynical, unpleasant atmosphere of the evening, Nick next meets Tom on a train going to New York City, and is dragged off to spend a drunken afternoon with Tom, his mistress Myrtle and their friends. It is clear that Tom has no intention of leaving Daisy for Myrtle, who is the wife of a humble garage keeper. She lived in a desolate area, a "valley of ashes", half-way between the Buchanan's West Egg home and New York City.

Nick attends one of Gatsby's huge parties and is intrigued by his host's melancholy aloofness. Nick learns gradually that Gatsby has been in love with Daisy for years; since an earlier involvement with her, he has nurtured a dream of winning her back from Tom with his newly amassed wealth. Nick and Jordan, who begin a low-key affair, arrange a meeting

Reprinted with permission of The Saturday Evening Post © 1920 renewed/The Curtis Publishing Company

WETTERAY

between Daisy and Gatsby.

Shy and terrified, Gatsby faces Daisy for the first time in almost five years. He takes her round his mansion, delighting in showing off the numerous rooms, wanting only that she should approve of him and like the mansion, the car, the clothes he has bought to impress her.

In love again, Daisy continues to visit Gatsby. She goes to one of his parties accompanied by Tom, who spends the evening criticizing Gatsby and threatening to find out how he made his money. Gatsby is desperate to recreate his past with Daisy. He believes she will divorce Tom and marry him. But week by week his dream slips further out of reach.

A showdown between Tom and Gatsby occurs one afternoon in an unbearably hot hotel room, when Gatsby urges Daisy to tell Tom she never loved him. "Oh you want too much!" she cries to Gatsby, unable to deny her early love

Detail from US recruiting poster/Imperial War Museum

The Kobal Collection

Across the bay
Gatsby's palatial house (left), opulent to a degree, stands across the bay from the Buchanans' home. "He had waited five years and bought a mansion where he dispensed star-light to casual moths" in a never-ending round of parties (above), in furtherance of a single ambition: to meet Daisy again.

but rather brutish Tom Buchanan.

Gatsby sets about making his millions with the sole aim of impressing her. The huge house, the parties, the shirts from London are all for her. He buys his mansion in West Egg to live across the bay from her, so that he can see the green light at the end of her dock. Now close to her, he is sure his dream will be fulfilled.

When he finally meets her again it is inevitable that his inflated dream must suffer from exposure to reality: " . . . the colossal vitality of his illusion . . . had gone beyond her, beyond everything. He had thrown himself into it with a creative passion, adding to it all the time, decking it out with every bright feather that drifted his way."

"'He's a bootlegger', said the young ladies, moving somewhere between his cocktails and his flowers. 'One time he killed a man who had found out that he was nephew to Von Hindenburg and second cousin to the devil. Reach me a rose, honey, and pour me a last drop into that there crystal glass.'"

Daisy tells Jordan
Gatsby was the man Daisy once knew, and Jordan recalls the young officer in Daisy's white car, five years ago.

for her husband. Gatsby becomes easy prey; Tom mercilessly exposes Gatsby's illicit means of acquiring wealth, until Daisy can bear to hear no more. The afternoon hurtles towards its appalling conclusion, leaving only Tom and Daisy unscathed.

'A SINGLE DREAM'
Jay Gatsby has become one of the great tragic heroes of 20th-century literature. Obsessed with creating vast wealth and an impressive image, in order to win back

his first love, he loses touch with everything in his past and finally with reality altogether.

The son of "shiftless and unsuccessful farm people", James Gatz was always ambitious. He left his family at the earliest opportunity and invented a new history and persona for himself. As Lieutenant Jay Gatsby, he met Daisy in 1917. She was out of his class and seemingly out of his reach, but they fell in love. When Gatsby went off to war, Daisy eventually tired of waiting and married the devoted

Illustrated London News Picture Library

A cool onlooker
Nick meets Jordan (above) at one of Gatsby's parties, watching the pleasure-seekers "with contemptuous interest".

He brings the same single-mindedness to bear on the present, insisting that everything can be made the same again – "Can't repeat the past? . . . Why of course you can!" His determination to wipe out everything from his and Daisy's life, apart from their love for each other, verges on the insane. He is unable to see her as she is, to believe she has had a child or ever loved her husband. Unable to inhabit the present, Gatsby becomes a non-person, a non-participator in his own parties, where no-one knows who he is.

MONEY AND CORRUPTION

The climactic scene in the hotel marks the separation between himself and Daisy. Gatsby refuses to let go of his early vision of her, even though it is clear to everyone else that she is no longer the fresh-faced girl of his dreams. Struggling to defend himself in the face of Tom's accusations of business corruption, he talks wildly to Daisy, "But with every word she was drawing further and further into herself, so he gave that up, and only the dead dream fought on as the afternoon slipped

In the Background

BOOTLEGGERS

Prohibition – the law banning the manufacture, sale and transport-ation of liquor in the US from 1920 to 1933 – proved impossible to enforce. People were prepared to pay high prices for illegal alcohol, and fortunes were made by those ready to supply it. The 'speakeasies' – illegal drinking clubs – made law-breaking positively fashionable.

The whisky run
A certain glamour was attached to the gangsters, racketeers and 'enterprising' individuals who ran risks to satisfy public demand for hard liquor – and to line their pockets (left). "A lot of these newly rich people are just big bootleggers", says Tom in The Great Gatsby. Gatsby himself is one such, although his motives for making money this way are more romantic than most.

away . . .". Gatsby has "paid a high price for living too long with a single dream".

The source of Gatsby's great wealth is obviously illegal. But the upper-class, idle rich, in the shape of Daisy and Tom Buchanan, are also corrupt:

"They were careless people, Tom and Daisy – they smashed up things and creatures and then retreated back into their money or their vast carelessness, or whatever it was that kept them together, and let other people clean up the mess they had made . . ."

Gatsby's dream is "incorruptible", but he himself is overwhelmed by external forces. Tom's "hard malice" and Daisy's "carelessness" are too much for him. His vast riches will never lift him into their

> "I thought of Gatsby's wonder when he first picked out the green light at the end of Daisy's dock. He had come a long way to this blue lawn, and his dream must have seemed so close that he could hardly fail to grasp it. He did not know that it was already behind him, somewhere back in that vast obscurity . . ."

"Daisy comes over"

Abruptly, the parties at Gatsby's place end. The house is silent, the servants have been replaced with 'discreet' henchmen, because "Daisy comes over quite often – in the afternoon". An affair has begun, and the world is no longer a welcome intruder.

able voice in the book. Revolted by the casual cruelty of the rich and famous, he comes to admire the straightforwardness of Gatsby's eternal search:

Through all he said, even through his appalling sentimentality, I was reminded of something – an elusive rhythm, a fragment of lost words, that I had heard somewhere a long time ago.

'A ROTTEN CROWD'

The elusive rhythm is perhaps a child-hood echo reaching back to the Middle West, which seems, in contrast to the East, to represent innocence, homely virtues and simplicity. Nick decides to return to his home, tired of the corrupt values and "quality of distortion" he has found in the East. The thought of Gatsby, with his unshakable loyalty to Daisy, prompts Nick to shout across the lawn towards the Gatsby mansion – "They're a rotten crowd . . . You're worth the whole damn bunch put together."

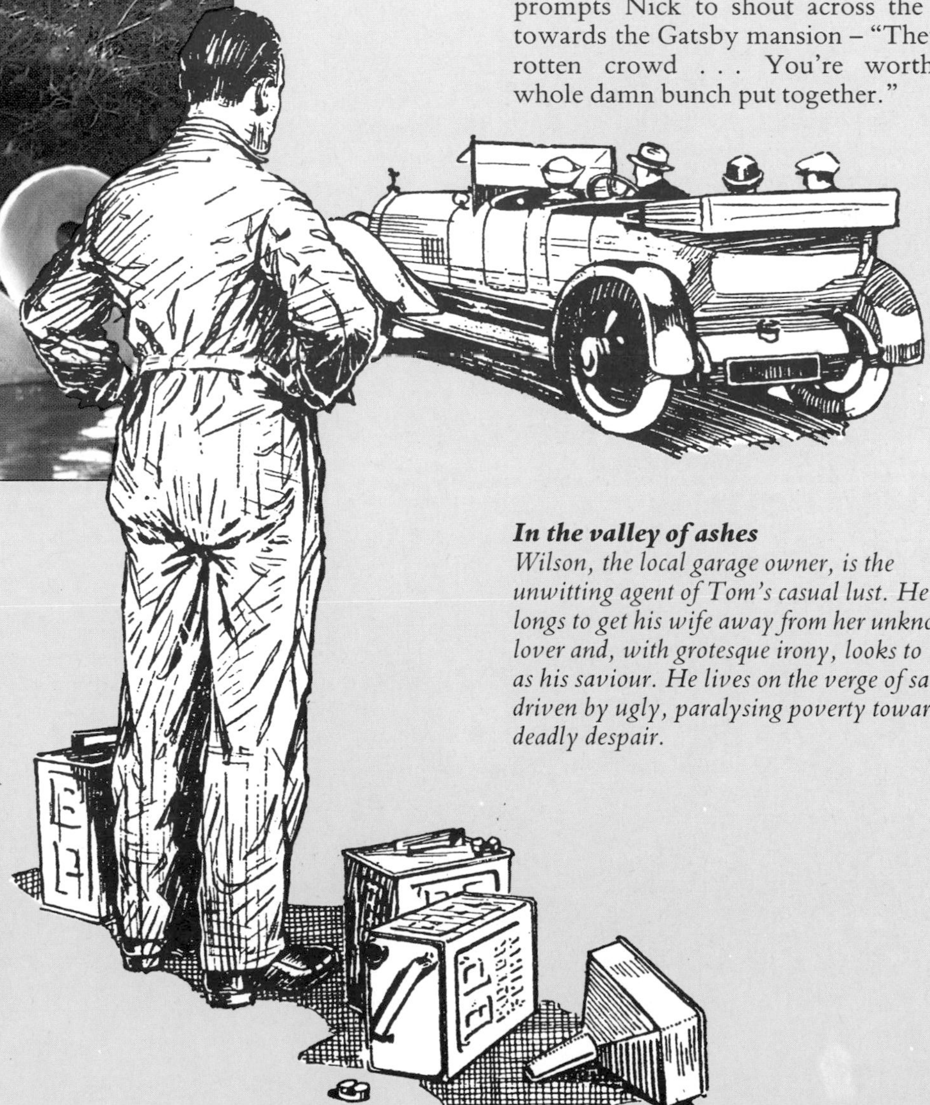

In the valley of ashes

Wilson, the local garage owner, is the unwitting agent of Tom's casual lust. He longs to get his wife away from her unknown lover and, with grotesque irony, looks to Tom as his saviour. He lives on the verge of sanity, driven by ugly, paralysing poverty towards deadly despair.

social milieu. His clothes are too vulgar, his display of wealth too ostentatious and his "elaborate formality of speech just missed being absurd". There is no room for Gatsby's sentimentality in the sophisticated cynical world of Tom and Daisy.

Gatsby somehow manages to retain a sort of purity to the end. But there is a stark contrast between the innocence of his dream and the dubious means whereby he has sought to realize it. The "foul dust that floated in the wake of his dreams covers him in the end" – but not before Nick, in penetrating the mystery of Gatsby, decides that he is, despite everything, "great".

Nick's judgement is the only morally reli-

Illustrated London News Picture Library

39

CHARACTERS IN FOCUS

The characters in *The Great Gatsby* have a symbolic significance beyond their function within the plot. Seen through Nick Carraway's eyes, they represent all that is dishonest and morally ugly. Their wealth and sophistication scarcely disguise their coarse brutality, vanity and selfishness. Only Gatsby in pursuit of his dream, and the essentially decent Nick himself, rise above the degeneracy.

WHO'S WHO

Nick Carraway An innocent from the Middle West, his tolerance and decency make him a reliable observer.

Jay Gatsby The enigmatic hero whose romantic sensitivity endears him to Nick, his neighbour in West Egg; a self-made man, driven by a single, overwhelming ambition.

Daisy Buchanan Rich, spoilt, world-weary and beautiful, Nick's "second cousin once removed" had "an excitement in her voice that men who had cared for her found difficult to forget."

Tom Buchanan Pompous, powerful and self-important, his reflex instinct is to cause pain. He is used to getting what he wants and gives "the appearance of always leaning aggressively forward".

Myrtle Wilson Tom's mistress, she is the complete opposite of Daisy. Her "intense vitality" and coarse sensuousness satisfy a deep need in him.

Wilson "Blond, spiritless . . . anaemic", he runs a garage amid ash heaps on the road to New York.

Jordan Baker A famous woman golfer doing the summer circuit of tournaments and dinner parties, she is also a charming, habitual liar.

Meyer Wolfsheim The sharp but sentimental businessman from the seedy underworld, who claims to have 'made' Gatsby.

"A sturdy straw-haired man of thirty, with a rather hard mouth and a supercilious manner", Tom Buchanan (right) is a hard-drinking, snobbish, rather stupid womanizer. A lifetime of success has made him a complete egotist. His brutish nature is expressed in his powerful, animal-fit body. "It was a body capable of enormous leverage – a cruel body."

Roger Coleman

S M Gerrard: Girl with Hat/Abbey Antiques, Hemel Hempstead/Bridgeman Art Library

An archetypal beauty of her class (above), Daisy is cool, perfumed, chic and full of frustrated boredom. However much she may still be in love with Gatsby, she will never leave the security and social status that are the bedrock of her life with Tom. "Her face was sad and lovely with bright things in it."

"I could see nothing sinister about him". Jay Gatsby (right), in spite of his shady background, is an intensely sympathetic figure possessing great personal charm; his smile has "a quality of eternal reassurance in it, that you come across four or five times in a life". The delight he takes in possessions and his longing to impress with them are almost childlike.

Roger Coleman

"I am inclined to reserve judgements", says Nick Carraway (left). The habit has "opened up many curious natures" to him. Jordan confides in him, Gatsby trusts him, Daisy feels safe to flirt with him. The reader, too, can trust his opinions: as he says, "I am one of the few honest people that I have ever known."

"In her middle thirties, and faintly stout", Myrtle Wilson (right) "carried her flesh sensuously as some women can . . . there was an immediate perceptible vitality about her as if all the nerves of her body were continually smouldering."

Illustrated London News Picture Library

Roger Coleman

Wilson (below) **"looked guilty, unforgivably guilty . . ."**, but has committed no sin except that of being poor and of loving a worthless wife with a fierce, inarticulate passion. The total disregard for his pain and poverty allows the tragic course of events to unfold.

Illustrated London News

41

BROKEN DREAMS

Despite a lifelong conviction that salvation lay only in hard, conscientious work, Fitzgerald frittered and drank his productive life away, redeeming it with a handful of masterpieces.

With his first novel, *This Side of Paradise* (1920), Scott Fitzgerald fixed his image in the American mind. He was the historian of 'the greatest, gaudiest spree in history' – the irresponsible good times of the 1920s, which he himself named 'the Jazz Age' and celebrated in tales of college boys, automobiles and flappers, youthful dreams and desires.

The rewards of such writing were great. Fitzgerald recalled that the Jazz Age 'bore him up, flattered him and gave him more money than he had dreamed of, simply for telling people that he felt as they did, that something had to be done with all the nervous energy stored up and unexpended in the War.'

For several years Fitzgerald deliberately exploited this profitable image, giving his earliest short-story collections the engagingly saleable titles of *Flappers and Philosophers* (1920) and *Tales of the Jazz Age* (1922). He adorned the *Tales* with

frivolous little commentaries, for example confessing that *The Camel's Back* had been written 'with the express purpose of buying a platinum and diamond wrist watch which cost six hundred dollars'. And, of course, Scott and Zelda's own alcoholic high jinks further reinforced the public image of Fitzgerald as a literary playboy.

The reality was quite different. *This Side of Paradise* appeared only after three years of intermittent rethinking and rewriting. And 'While I waited for the novel to appear, the metamorphosis of amateur into professional began to take place – a sort of stitching together of your whole life into a pattern of work, so that the end of one job is automatically the beginning of another.' Except in his very darkest periods Fitzgerald remained a professional, painstaking even when compelled to undertake frenzied story-writing to pay off debts or to finance some new departure. Any work he cared about was usually drafted in pencil, then typed,

Wallace Irwin – Hugh Wiley – F. Scott Fitzgerald – Harrison Rh Graeve – Henry C. Rowland – Thomas Joyce – Hal G. E

Regular income
The Saturday Evening Post *(above right) was a regular, remunerative outlet, but was costly of time Fitzgerald might have spent on 'serious' writing.*

Playing Triangle
Fitzgerald won his way into the prestigious Princeton Triangle drama club (left) with the plot and lyrics of a musical. On nationwide tour reviews said he 'could take his place right now with the brightest writers of witty lyrics in America'. When he missed Presidency of the Club, he 'set about learning how to write' instead.

revised and retyped at least twice. He told one of his secretaries, 'Yes, three drafts are absolutely necessary. First, the high inspirational points. Second, the cold going over. Third, putting both in their proper perspective'.

'LIFE IS TOO STRONG'

Nor was Fitzgerald's outlook as light-hearted as many of his contemporaries believed. Even in 1920, his wonder-year, he declared that 'life is too strong and remorseless for the sons of men'; and, from the very beginning, the same conviction lurked behind the wit and wild high spirits of his writings. It is one of the oddest things about Fitzgerald that he was enchanted by and caught up in the carnival of the 1920s, while – as a writer – he sensed its flawed nature and imminent dissolution. 'All the stories that came into my head had a touch of disaster in them – the lovely young creatures in my novels went to ruin, the diamond mountains of my short stories blew up, my millionaires were as beautiful and damned as Thomas Hardy's peasants. In life these things hadn't happened yet, but I was pretty sure living wasn't the reckless, careless

Rich pickings
Fitzgerald's subject-matter – Riviera partying (below) and the frivolous rich (right) – gave his readers a vicarious share in the Good Life while assuring them of its sad, destructive pointlessness.

business people thought.'

Fitzgerald's second novel, *The Beautiful and Damned* (1922), sounded a still more sombre note, showing the destructive effects of false values on Anthony and Gloria, the archetypal college boy and flapper. From this time onwards, in fact, Fitzgerald's essential subject would not be the Bright Young Things but 'All the Sad Young Men' – and women – whose romantic dreams broke apart when they were put to the test in the real world. Its most complex, concentrated and poetic formulation would be *The Great Gatsby* (1925), in which both the reality and the

dreams came under Fitzgerald's scrutiny.

The poet T. S. Eliot hailed *Gatsby* as 'the first step that American fiction has taken since Henry James', and many of Fitzgerald's other fellow-writers were equally complimentary. But the public response was less enthusiastic, and by Fitzgerald's standards the initial sale of 22,000 copies was poor. The brevity of the book was against it. Many readers failed to appreciate the way in which Fitzgerald had implied rather than spelled out certain facets of the story (for example, the murky underworld history on which Jay Gatsby's social eminence is built). And despite its frantic parties, *Gatsby* was not the sort of novel that people expected from the author of *Flappers and Philosophers*.

Fitzgerald's image became even more of a handicap during the 1930s, when the Wall Street Crash of 1929 and the Great Depression altered the public mood. The Jazz Age was over, and Fitzgerald began to seem like an outmoded figure – a misfortune compounded by Zelda's breakdown only a few months after the Crash. His own crisis of confidence culminated

43

Celluloid fame
*The Great Gatsby
was filmed three
times – in 1926,
1949 and 1974. The
second version (left)
shows curiously
incongruous dress.
Fitzgerald's
scriptwriting earned
him only one credit –
for* The Three
Comrades *(right).
Exhaustion marks
the writer's face by
the thirties (below).*

in the discovery that 'The conjurer's hat
was empty'.

After eight years and 17 drafts, *Tender is
the Night* (1934) was published but failed
either to sell in large numbers or to re-
establish Fitzgerald's now flagging reputation. By the late 1930s, when he wanted
to present Sheilah Graham with a set of
his works, most bookshops no longer
stocked them; and all too many of the
people he met stared at Fitzgerald in surprise, having assumed that he had died
some years before. At the time of his fatal
heart attack he had not published a novel
for six years, and despite a few perceptive
obituaries it was left to posterity to recog-
nize the permanent value of his work.

SQUANDERED TALENT

Scott Fitzgerald took terrible risks with
his talent. The Fitzgeralds' reckless, high-
spending way of life made novel-writing
a luxury he could indulge only between
long 'intervals of trash' – the magazine
stories for which he was paid up to $4,000
by the *Saturday Evening Post*. (Some of his
best stories, including *May Day* and *The
Diamond as Big as the Ritz*, failed to suit
this market and had to be sold elsewhere
for much smaller sums.) Fitzgerald himself ruefully admitted that 'I have been
only a mediocre caretaker of the things
left in my hands, even of my talent.'

Yet the talent itself survived, full of a
poetic intensity and evocative emotional
quality rare among novelists. At the darkest moments in his career, Fitzgerald
wrote about his inability to write – brief,
poignant confessional essays such as 'The
Crack-Up' and *Afternoon of an Author*. And,
with *The Last Tycoon*, he at last recovered
the discipline and dedication needed to
tackle a novel – one that remains a brilliant and tantalizing fragment, since
Fitzgerald's heart succumbed to stress
more readily than his much-abused but
ultimately indestructible talent.

The immediate success of Scott Fitzgerald's first novel, *This Side of Paradise* (1920), established him as the celebrant of 'flaming youth' – an image he exploited in his *Tales of the Jazz Age* (1922). But although he was dazzled by the glamour and the pleasure of the 'sweet life', Fitzgerald also sensed the fragile, corruptible nature of American dreams, chronicling their extinction in *The Beautiful and Damned* (1922), *The Great Gatsby* (1925) and *All the Sad Young Men* (1926). After a long, unproductive gap, he completed one more novel, *Tender is the Night* (1934), drawing extensively on his knowledge of the Riviera and Zelda's psychiatric treatment. Personally and creatively derelict for most of the 1930s, he capitalized on his own difficulties by writing autobiographical pieces, collected in *The Crack-Up* (1945). His unfinished, posthumously published novel of Hollywood, *The Last Tycoon* (1941), shows the late return of his creative powers.

THIS SIDE OF PARADISE
◆1920◆

A new type of American girl (right) invites the attentions of 'romantic egotist' Amory Blaine. After making his mark on Princeton University's literary and social scene, Amory embarks on his first sexual adventure with a woman who smokes, drinks and is willing to pet in automobiles. After a spell in the Army, he returns to find his mother dead and his income sadly reduced. When he falls passionately for debutante Rosalind Connage, she simply cannot envisage happiness without money . . . This novel, by a very young Fitzgerald, is a mix of autobiography and wish-fulfilment.

Illustrated London News Picture Library

THE BEAUTIFUL AND DAMNED
◆1922◆

Gifted Harvard man Anthony Patch pursues and marries the lovely Gloria (below). But it soon becomes plain that for all his fashionable and philosophical talk, he is simply marking time until he inherits his grandfather's fortune. He claims his life of inertia is a conscious refusal to give in to the sordid world. But the grandfather breaks in on one of their riotous parties and disinherits Anthony and Gloria. They deteriorate in their own ways, and Anthony's life is seen in increasing contrast to that of successful cinema director Joseph Bloeckman.

TALES OF THE JAZZ AGE

◆ 1922 ◆

The Camel's Back *is pure comedy* – in which
a man goes in fancy dress to the wrong party
(above). But Fitzgerald's second collection of
short stories encompasses a variety of different
moods and styles. In the sombre *Lees of
Happiness*, a woman's life is destroyed when a
blood clot bursts in her husband's brain. *May
Day* describes the criss-crossing of several
lives in a single day – bringing drunken revelry
to some, death and shame to others. And *The
Diamond as Big as the Ritz*, an unusual,
tongue-in-cheek fantasy, is Fitzgerald's single
most famous story.

ALL THE SAD YOUNG MEN

◆ 1926 ◆

'Story about Zelda and me. All true', wrote
Fitzgerald of *The Sensible Thing:* George
O'Kelly is thrown over by a small-town belle
who feels she can wait no longer for him to
make a brilliant success (right). Within the
year he returns in triumph to win her back –
though a certain April romance has gone for
ever from his heart. Similar loss and disillusion
haunt this third collection of Fitzgerald's
stories. One scene intended for inclusion in
The Great Gatsby turns up under the title
Absolution.

TENDER IS THE NIGHT
◆1934◆

Dick and Nicole Diver seem the ideal couple (below), moving with ease through the sophisticated society of the Riviera. But the Divers' happiness is extremely fragile. Nicole is the former patient of Dick, once a gifted psychiatrist, who was treating her for schizophrenia, caused by her incestuous relationship with her father. Her wealthy family allowed the marriage, seeing Diver as a convenient minder for their deranged daughter. Now he has been drawn into a glamorously vacuous way of life that has destroyed his urge to work and is slowly corrupting him physically and mentally. The action is seen through the eyes of a young movie star, Rosemary Hoyt. At first Nicole's dependency on Dick gives his life some meaning, and he can resist the allure of Rosemary. But as Nicole recovers, and Dick relies more and more on drink, the roles of dependency gradually become reversed . . . The novel is especially poignant because it reflects so much of Scott and Zelda's lives.

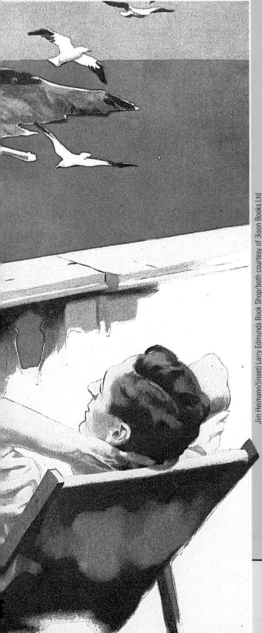

THE CRACK-UP
◆1945◆

When Scott Fitzgerald and his marriage had 'cracked like an old plate' (right), he recorded the phenomenon in the poignant title–piece of this collection, published posthumously. Its essays, stories, notes and letters were edited by his friend, the critic Edmund Wilson. *Echoes of the Jazz Age* is an elegy for the 10-year American spree that ended with the Wall Street Crash. *My Lost City* surveys Fitzgerald's changing view of New York during the same period. *Early Success* is even more directly autobiographical and explores how success changed Fitzgerald's life after the publication of *This Side of Paradise*. *Sleeping and Waking* describes insomniac nights in his difficult later years, when he was writing *Tender is the Night*.

THE LAST TYCOON
◆1941◆

In the 1930s, Hollywood was the world's dream factory (below). Monroe Stahr, 'the last tycoon', is a producer of genius, celebrated for his inspired, incisive decision-making. His story is seen through the eyes of Cecilia Brady, a college girl in love with him. Stahr, mourning his dead wife, is unresponsive. He simply works ceaselessly, with dangerous intensity. But when an earth tremor floods the studios, Stahr sees two girls floating by on one of the props – a giant head of the Indian goddess Siva. One of the girls, the young, complex Kathleen, reminds him of his late wife Minna and threatens his insularity. Stahr's future will depend on whether he can bring his famous powers of direction to bear on the drama of his private life.

Bettmann Archive Inc/BBC Hulton Picture Library

Jim Heimann/(inset) Larry Edmunds Book Shop/both courtesy of Bison Books Ltd

THE JAZZ AGE

Drinking, dancing and madcap parties – the Jazz Age had them all. Excess was the order of the day – but burn-out, as for Scott and Zelda Fitzgerald, came early.

Fitzgerald enjoyed a unique relationship with the 1920s. He labelled the era 'the Jazz Age' and then conducted his life as a public explanation of what he meant by the phrase. In a sense, therefore, Fitzgerald and the Jazz Age are wrapped up together in a way that is unusual, perhaps even unprecedented, for a writer and his period.

In 1926, a year after publishing *The Great Gatsby,* the author cast a jaundiced eye over the New York social scene just past. 'The restlessness approached hysteria. The parties were bigger. The pace was faster, the shows were broader, the buildings were higher, the morals were looser, and the liquor was cheaper; but all these benefits did not really minister to much delight. Young people wore out early – they were hard and languid at twenty-one. Most of my friends drank too much – the more they were in tune to the times the more they drank . . .'

Scott and Zelda were, by this yardstick, absolutely in tune with the times. Their thirst was legendary, and they themselves did wear out sadly early. Beyond that irony, however, Fitzgerald's barbed comment goes straight to the heart of the Jazz Age and his relationship with it.

He sees fun everywhere and pleasure nowhere. Everyone has been to parties that leave a rather sour taste the morning after, but for sheer pointlessness Jay Gatsby's elaborate binges would take a lot of beating. Why the cynical tone which seems to permeate the Jazz Age?

THE 'LOST GENERATION'
The avant-garde writer Gertrude Stein once told Ernest Hemingway that his was a 'lost generation'. Apparently she said it partly in jest, but she was near enough the mark for the term to become a lasting catchphrase. Members of the Lost Generation had, by this reckoning, been permanently scarred by the Great War, even if some (like Fitzgerald) had not seen action. They felt rootless because they were cut off from the values of a time remembered by the great divide of the war, and cynical because the carnage had crushed natural youthful idealism. Jay Gatsby's deliberately obscured origins exaggerate this sense of rootlessness, and this serves to make him a particularly poignant representative of the Lost Generation. So too are Tom and Daisy examples, if less attractive ones. And so were Fitzgerald and Zelda.

Outsmarting the law
Prohibition spawned ingenious counter-measures. The woman (left) dons a baggy overcoat to conceal tins of illicit booze, while the infamous gangster Al Capone (above right) operated on a larger scale, organizing his mob to stop at nothing to quench the nation's thirst. Occasionally, though, Prohibition agents got lucky. In a coal steamer in New York harbour (right) they found hidden a cache of some 3000 bottles of liquor.

of the prohibitionists for the law, the passion of the drinking classes for drink, and the passion of the largest and best-organized smuggling trade that has ever existed for money'.

The 'drys' had completely misread the American temper, indeed human nature. Instead of inspiring a moral revival, spearheaded by universal sobriety, they triggered an obsession with alcohol. Books, newspapers and magazines were filled with descriptions and discussions of drink, while cartoonists attacked the subject with glee. To the pleasures of drinking were now added a frisson of danger and the thrill of getting away with it, of outwitting the law.

Ingenuity in concealing drink knew no bounds. Large, floppy overcoats had obvious attractions, and so did stylish Russian boots with their baggy tops. The hip-flask became a natural accessory to dress, while the more imaginative might savour the delights dispensed by a hollow walking-stick. A good-sized baby buggy could conceal a still, with baby perched innocently on top. And in one reported incident, an imaginative fellow was caught at the Canadian border with a few dozen eggs – each carefully drained and filled with liquor.

There was, however, a darker side to the Prohibition experience that would remain a stain on the American landscape long after Prohibition itself had become just a distant, whimsical memory. For an illicit liquor trade to flourish it required a three-cornered conspiracy. The drinker wanted his drink and convivial surroundings in which to consume it. He cared little – if at all – that he was encouraging crime and lining the pockets of criminals in order to get it. And he did not take kindly to special Federal agents or zealous police-

The idea of a spiritual void may seem incongruous as a backdrop to the Roaring Twenties – as the decade was also known – but the incongruity is superficial. The immediate post-war years were marked in both Britain and Europe by hectic gaiety, as youthful survivors turned their backs on a devastated past. And after what they had just been through, what price the future? Hence the cynicism, and hence the jaunty, flippant, carefree defiance with which they attacked the present.

PROHIBITION

In the United States, much of the defiance was directed at the question of drinking – or rather, not drinking. On 16 January 1920, the Eighteenth Amendment to the Constitution came into effect, prohibiting the manufacture, sale or transport of intoxicating liquor. This extraordinary piece of legislation had come about as a result of decades of lobbying by the Temperance Movement, and it represented a last-ditch stand by the forces of an older, rural America against the more sophisticated, 'sinful' city folk.

The 'noble experiment' of 'purifying' the nation was a spectacular failure. As quickly as the saloons were boarded up, speakeasies (liquor shops) threw open their doors (ever on the look-out for Prohibition agents). Moonshining – the illicit distilling of alcohol, which was formerly a quaint old hillbilly custom – became big business overnight as bootleggers rushed to satisfy the needs of thirsty Americans. Huge quantities of liquor were smuggled in from Canada and Mexico. As one wag put it in 1924, Prohibition had the merit of satisfying 'three tremendous popular passions – the passion

Razzmatazz

(above) From the pulsating throb of the dance floor to the blood lust of the boxing ring, cities exuded the energy – and excesses – of the age.

Music by Gershwin

Known primarily for his Rhapsody in Blue, *George Gershwin showed just how 'serious' jazz rhythms could be in the hands of a symphonic genius. For four years from 1920 he wrote music for George White's Scandals – a rival dance company to the spectacular Ziegfeld Follies.*

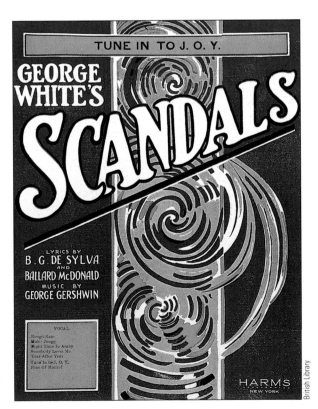

TUNE IN TO J. O. Y.

GEORGE WHITE'S

SCANDALS

LYRICS BY
B. G. DE SYLVA
AND
BALLARD McDONALD
MUSIC BY
GEORGE GERSHWIN

VOCAL.

Kongo Kate
Mah-Jongg
Night Time In Araby
Somebody Loves Me.
Year-After-Year
Tune In to J. O. Y.
Blare Of Madrid

HARMS
NEW YORK

Sources and Inspiration

RUDOLPH VALENTINO & VILMA BANKY. 236.P.
IN "THE SON OF THE SHEIK".
'FAMOUS CINEMA STAR' SERIES.

Mary Evans Picture Library

A nation's heart-throb
(left) The silent movie stars of the twenties thrilled audiences disillusioned by the war years who wanted to believe in magic, romance, and tales with happy endings.

All that jazz
A black creation and originally the music of the poor, jazz spread slowly upriver from its New Orleans source. The young Louis Armstrong (centre, right), a self-taught and brilliantly talented orphan, made his name with 'King Oliver's Creole Jazz Band'.

Sporting heroes
Sport provided another arena for escapism. The tennis stars Bill Tilden and Helen Wills (below) had all of America rooting for them during their Wimbledon appearances.

BBC Hulton Picture Library

men who smashed up their stills, confiscated their smuggled, good-quality liquor and raided their premises – nor the distinct possibility of being hauled before the law as the result of a raid.

The illegal liquor trade was an irresistible lure to the most avaricious and ruthless criminal elements in the land. The money to be made was colossal, and it was absurd to imagine that serious crooks would not take advantage of this unprecedented opportunity. There did remain a cottage-industry element in bootlegging, however, neatly expressed in a jolly parody of *My bonny lies over the ocean:*

Mother makes brandy from cherries,
Pop distills whisky and gin,
Sister sells wine from the grapes on our vine.
Oh Lord how the money rolls in!

Right from the start, moreover, otherwise law-abiding citizens were in open collusion with big-time criminals in attempting to thwart the law. Al Capone, the biggest hoodlum of them all, put his finger on this hypocrisy by once posing the question, 'What's Al Capone done, then? He's supplied a legitimate demand. Some call it bootlegging. Some call it racketeering. I call it a business. They say I violate the Prohibition law. Who doesn't?'

The third corner of the triangle was the law itself, in the shape of those charged with the responsibility for enforcing it. There were many incorruptible Prohibition agents and ordinary policemen, some of them heroically so, but gener-

ally the law was applied haphazardly, and corruption was rife. With a hostile public on the one hand, and easy bribes on the other, many policemen took the softer, more lucrative option.

Prohibition, then, which was a sincere attempt to improve public morals, backfired completely. It led to a reckless approach to drinking, a casual contempt for the law, widespread police corruption and the permanent blight of organized crime as a feature of big-city American life.

Jay Gatsby is a successful racketeer of an unspecified sort, but his criminality is peripheral

The Keystone Collection

The Keystone Collection

50

to become a world-wide legend. The performers and composers who rose to fame in the 1920s form a galaxy of musical brilliance: the haunting blues singer Bessie Smith; the ebullient Jelly Roll Morton and his 'Red Hot Peppers'; the incomparable Duke Ellington whose career as a front-rank composer, band leader and pianist was to span half a century; plus the white composers Irving Berlin, Jerome Kern and George Gershwin.

The Jazz Age was also the age of sport, in the sense that it witnessed the emergence of big-time, big-money sport across a wide spectrum. Baseball, America's national game, had long been professional and highly popular, but its reputation had been tarnished in 1919 by a true incident used in *The Great Gatsby* – the Chicago White Sox scandal, in which a game was rigged for money. The image of sport recovered in the Twenties, mainly through the prodigious batting feats of Babe Ruth. The 'Sultan of Swat' and his New York Yankees were a national institution, and it is some measure of his fame that his name still rings a bell – virtually anywhere – with those who know nothing of baseball and care nothing for sport.

What Ruth was to baseball, Jack Dempsey was to professional boxing. Initially unpopular because he had not served during the War, the 'Manassa Mauler' ruled the heavyweight roost from 1919 to 1926. Millions followed his ring exploits through the sporting pages and via the great new popular medium of radio. Even today, many who take an interest in boxing hold Dempsey in awe, as do golfers the immortal Bobby Jones. The tennis players Bill Tilden and Helen Wills and

to the lives of those around him, just as crime was peripheral to the lives of most people during the Jazz Age. They may have quaffed bootleg booze, but pay-offs and shakedowns and gangland murders were just things they read about in the newspapers. They wanted to look on the bright side of life, and if they were young, fit and reasonably affluent they could find plenty of that on offer. Indeed, though few could afford the Gatsby lifestyle, jobs were plentiful, wages were high and most of the fun things to do were cheap enough to come within reach of all but the very poor.

Suddenly everyone appeared to own a car, and everyone could and did go to the movies and listen to the radio and the gramophone. Dancing was all the rage, and the young flapper and her beau had the new-found freedom to step out for a night on the town unchaperoned.

JAZZ RHYTHMS

Fitzgerald chose to name the age for the music it danced and listened to – that irresistible synthesis of negro spirituals, work songs and blues which suddenly caught the American (and European) imagination around the beginning of the decade. Jazz was largely confined to the red-light district of Storyville, New Orleans, until the US Navy police closed Storyville down in 1917. Jazz bands and musicians then made their way up the Mississippi, establishing themselves in Memphis, St Louis, Louisville and Chicago.

While the new music quickly swept east and west, Chicago remained the jazz headquarters during the 1920s. 'King Oliver's Creole Jazz Band' was the best in the business, and its sensational young trumpet-player Louis Armstrong went on

Conquering the air
Charles Lindbergh, once known as the 'flying fool' for his airborne antics, winged his way into people's hearts and made aviation history with his first solo flight across the Atlantic in 1927. The New York to Paris run took him 33½ hours, won him $25,000 in prize money, and made him a household name. The world rejoiced – suddenly anything was possible.

The new woman
Faster, freer and intent on having a good time, the twenties woman flashed thigh and flouted convention in a single-minded pursuit of happiness.

Bettmann Archive Inc/BBC Hulton Picture Library

Danced off her feet
Dance marathons, with the lure of big money prizes for the couple that could keep going the longest, drew young hopefuls from miles around. Couples bopped till they dropped, literally, and one marathon went on for a staggering 17 weeks.

The Wall Street Crash
Millions of people lost their life's savings in the Wall Street Crash of 1929. Banks folded, the stock market collapsed and with unemployment sweeping the nation the Jazz Age came to its end.

Along with hero worship went an inexhaustible appetite for fads and ballyhoo. For some it was crossword puzzles, Mah-Jong and bridge; for others yo-yos, pogo sticks and roller-skates. More extreme were crazes like flagpole sitting, and while this was, mercifully, only a minority participant sport, the 'sitters' drew vast crowds. The most famous of them, 'Shipwreck' Kelly, spent nearly five months astride various flagpoles in 1929, his peak year.

Dance marathons also had a vogue, and these could be dangerous as well as foolish. They went on for days, often weeks, and on one occasion in Chicago reached an incredible 119 days.

The Jazz Age was an age of excitement and of excess. People lived hard, played hard, and burnt out early. Cynicism came to replace confidence; disillusionment replaced the razzmatazz. And with the Wall Street Crash of 1929 and the ensuing Great Depression, Fitzgerald and millions of other Americans had to face a grimmer kind of reality as the new decade dawned.

the American footballer Red Grange were equally celebrated, and together with a host of other great competitors in all disciplines they contributed to a golden age of sport.

Hero worship was a notable characteristic of the age, and celebrities could be found in any field of entertainment. Silent movie stars like Charlie Chaplin and Douglas Fairbanks, Fairbanks' wife Mary Pickford and the 'It' girl, Clara Bow, were hugely popular, especially if sexual innuendo was involved. Rudolf Valentino was mobbed by screaming women whenever he had the temerity to appear in public, and when 'The Sheik' died, suddenly and prematurely in 1926, he was mourned by millions of heart-broken fans.

'LUCKY LINDY'

Perhaps the greatest hero of the age, however, had nothing to do with the entertainment industry. Charles Lindbergh was a young aviator who had honed his skills as a barnstorming pilot in the middle-western states. On 20 May 1927 at 7 am he took off from New York in a little monoplane named the *Spirit of St Louis* in an attempt to win a $25,000 prize for the first non-stop flight across the Atlantic to Paris. After 33½ hours 'Lucky Lindy' touched down at Le Bourget, to be greeted by 100,000 ecstatic French spectators. He returned to New York to a hero's welcome of delirious proportions. In the course of a tickertape parade an estimated 1800 tons of paper and confetti showered down from office windows overhead.

Giancarlo Costa

JOHN STEINBECK

1902 - 1968

Shunning publicity and the encumbrances of success, John
Steinbeck devoted himself to his work, to understanding the
inner man, to fighting – in his life as in his writing – for the
causes he believed in. In so doing – in championing the poor,
the unemployed, the persecuted – he created fiction which
assured him a well deserved place in the ranks of America's
greats. The Nobel Prize in 1962 acknowledged the greatness
that his readers had recognized for decades.

ONLY ONE COMMANDMENT

Acute observation and a full life convinced Steinbeck that there is 'only one commandment for living things: Survive!' But he retained an intense, humane faith in Society's potential.

A love for the sea
Steinbeck called the Pacific (above) his 'home ocean': it gave him 'a kind of boisterous joy'. Later, however, he made his home on the East (Atlantic) Coast.

Small-town beginnings
Salinas (above left) had grown at a crossroads, at the end of a valley in California's coastal mountains. It was a small town with not more than two and a half thousand inhabitants and, to John, a living personality.

John and Olive Steinbeck
(left) An ex-teacher, John's mother Olive was an educated, strong, capable and cheerful woman, deeply proud of her son, the writer. His father John was a strict, demanding, silent man whose expectations the son found hard to satisfy.

S teinbeck learned that he had won the 1962 Nobel Prize for Literature from a breakfast television news report. That afternoon he faced 150 reporters. "Do you really think you deserve the Nobel Prize?" asked one brash journalist. "Frankly, no", answered Steinbeck. His reply was the level-headed assessment of an honest man, whose ego rarely got in the way of his judgement. Though a writer by nature, inclination and ambition, he had done so many other jobs, seen so many aspects of life other than the artistic one, that his own literary achievements did not seem momentous to him. And shyness made the role of celebrity thoroughly unwelcome.

John Ernst Steinbeck was born in Salinas, California, on 27 February, 1902, the third of four children, and the only boy. His father, also John Ernst, was an accountant and the treasurer of Monterey County; his mother, Olive, was a former school teacher. In spite of this respectable background, young John was socially awkward and inclined to be reclusive. A big, shambling boy, he did not excel at sport and was too shy to succeed with girls at high school. But he did have a gift for

Spectrum Colour Library

academic discipline. He took what courses he chose – mainly writing, literature, history and the classics – and once battled unsuccessfully to take a medical course on the dissection of corpses because he 'wanted to know more about people'. As he worked only at what he enjoyed, he teetered on the edge of failure during much of his university career. He attended classes intermittently over a period of six years, but never took a degree.

The rest of the time he worked at a series of jobs on ranches and fruit farms and in sugar factories, learning as much from the poor Mexicans with whom he lived as from his privileged classmates at Stanford. This dual education gave Steinbeck the remarkable sympathy and breadth of perception that distinguish his best work. Out in the fields or factories, his heart bled for the ignorant and deprived among whom he worked. Once, forced to attend church with a friend's family, he grew incensed by the complacent sermon. 'Feed the body and the soul will take care of itself!' he shouted at the astonished preacher.

A REBELLIOUS INTELLECT

Steinbeck left Stanford a tall, well-built young man, still bearishly independent, but respected by his fellow students for his rebellious intellect, as well as for his overriding desire to write. He was already becoming a very competent writer, but his first assignment as a newspaper reporter in New York was short-lived. He was dismissed for incompetence from the staff of the *American* after a very brief trial period. (He got lost while out on stories, he later claimed.) He probably contributed more to New York as a labourer working on the construction of Madison Square gardens.

Steinbeck retreated to California – to Lake Tahoe, where he was employed for two seasons as a winter caretaker. There, among the snowdrifts,

telling stories, and from his early teens he determined to become a writer. Neighbours remember him, hour on end, sitting at the window of his upstairs room, apparently staring across the street – lost in a daydream world in which he was to wander throughout much of his adult life.

Steinbeck was admitted to Stanford University, California, in 1919, but was fiercely resistant to

Courtesy of the John Steinbeck Archives

Salinas High School
(left) Shy, unpopular, aloof and rather lazy, Steinbeck – pictured far right, back row – just managed to achieve the above-average grades his family expected of him.

Carol Henning
(right) 'She satisfies me in many ways for she is lovely and clever and passionate . . .' Carol proved a devoted wife, sharing penury and uncertainty with Steinbeck and subordinating herself to his demanding nature. She was shattered when the marriage ended.

Richard Albee, Courtesy of the Steinbeck Library

he had in his life. In 1948, when Ed was killed, Steinbeck wrote, "There died the greatest man I have known and the best teacher."

In 1931 Steinbeck began a lifelong and affectionate relationship with the firm of (Mavis) McIntosh and (Elizabeth) Otis, literary agents. Through these two enlightened women he found publishers for two more novels. And during the next two difficult years, when both his mother and father died, he wrote a book that brought him money and notoriety. For the rest of his life he would be both solvent and famous. *Tortilla Flat* was a light-hearted treatment of the *paisanos,* the Mexican Californians whom Steinbeck knew so well. Although denounced by the Chamber of Commerce in Monterey, where Tortilla Flat was reputed to exist, the book became a best-seller.

THE PERILS OF FAME

Fame, according to Steinbeck, was 'a pain in the ass', and unlike many writers, he meant it. Resisting the temptation to lay aside his pencils and become a zoologist, he wrote in quick succession three novels upon which his reputation securely stands: *In Dubious Battle, Of Mice and Men* and *The Grapes of Wrath.* These were all books about destitute people – people with whom Steinbeck deeply sympathized, although his understanding was misinterpreted on all sides. Farm owners and conservative politicians thought him a Marxist subversive, while the intellectual Left vilified him for stopping short of Communist commitment. Such was the abuse and controversy surrounding *The Grapes of Wrath* that Steinbeck rejoiced when it finally slipped from the best-seller list.

John and Carol Steinbeck, suddenly wealthy but no longer happy, began to drift apart. He found a new love in Gwyndolyn Conger, a professional singer. Steinbeck could not bear to keep the affair

he completed his first, ambitious novel, *Cup of Gold,* which was published in 1929. And while working at a nearby fish hatchery, he met Carol Henning, whom he married.

Faced with domestic responsibilities and the catastrophe of the Depression, Steinbeck put his head down, sharpened his pencils (about two dozen every morning) and continued to write fiction. He and Carol lived in his parents' beach house at Pacific Grove, partly supported by his father, who respected John's determination.

Steinbeck's penurious life at Pacific Grove was enriched and changed when he met Ed Ricketts. Ed ran the Pacific Biological Laboratory in nearby Monterey, supplying schools and institutions with a variety of creatures, living or dead, from cats to cuttlefish. Steinbeck had always been fascinated by the natural world; at university he had once kept a canary, a chipmunk and a turtle in his room, and he had studied zoology at Hopkins Marine Station one summer. But Ed had more than one interest in common with Steinbeck. He was a serious thinker and a persuasive talker, who confirmed Steinbeck's belief that mankind was an integral part of the animal kingdom, not a separate species working out some divine plan. Steinbeck's friendship with Ed was as close as any relationship

New York City
Young Steinbeck arrived in New York (above) with three dollars and 'a touch of panic in my stomach'. He pushed barrows of concrete, then half-starved as a reporter. Later, he returned there a celebrity, with his third wife, to a house on 72nd Street.

Famous friends
With growing wealth and increasing connections with Hollywood, Steinbeck and Carol formed a new circle of friends – he called them 'the swimming pool set' – but some deeper friendships began, with Spencer Tracy (right), for instance, who starred in the film of Tortilla Flat.

a secret and told Carol; but she was determined not to give up her husband. The conflict brought Steinbeck to the verge of a nervous breakdown. He wrote, 'I don't know why in hell anybody would want to bother with me. Anyway, Carol won the outside and G the inside, and I don't seem able to get put back together.' He finally married Gwyn in 1943.

Few writers have weathered such an avalanche of success as did Steinbeck between 1935 and America's entry into the War in 1941. His own dramatized version of *Of Mice and Men* was a hit on Broadway, while *The Grapes of Wrath* won him a Pulitzer Prize in 1940. He was also elected to the National Institute of Arts and Letters. Hollywood meanwhile courted him assiduously; while dodging autograph hunters and gossip columnists Steinbeck saw four of his novels become films in as many years. And although he hated the paraphernalia of fame, his involvement with films brought him the friendship of actors such as Spencer Tracy and Henry Fonda.

WAR EFFORTS

Steinbeck described World War II with typical detachment – 'part of a species pattern', he called it – but threw himself into the war effort with enthusiasm. Fascinated by propaganda, he tried to persuade President Roosevelt to litter Germany with counterfeit paper money dropped from the air. He also wrote the story and screenplay *Bombs Away* in praise of the Air Force (and because he wanted to fly in a bomber). His struggles to obtain a civilian commission in the army, however, were fruitless; in the eyes of the Establishment he was 'apparently communistic'.

Finally he took a job as correspondent with the *New York Herald Tribune*, travelling to North Africa and on to Italy with the Allied invasion. In

THE GREATEST MAN IN THE WORLD

The small-town marine biologist and philosopher Ed Ricketts appears thinly disguised in three of Steinbeck's books; the writer clearly idolized this unaligned free-thinker. They collaborated on *Sea of Cortez* (1941, non-fiction) after an excursion in the Gulf of California. When, on a Cannery Row level crossing, Ed's car was hit by a train, and he lay for four days dying, Steinbeck wept, 'The greatest man in the world is dying and there is nothing I can do.'

War writer
Steinbeck had himself posted to a top secret US naval unit (above) led by friend Douglas Fairbanks Jr. The film adaptation of The Moon is Down *(1942) (inset) was accused in America of romanticizing the enemy. But the book was an inspiration to the resistance in Denmark, where to own a copy was punishable by death.*

Gwyndolyn the goddess
Steinbeck worshipped his second wife (pictured right with their son John) with an unrealistic fervour. Whether she, he or both of them changed, she wrote that for 'one solid year after he came back from the war he had no sense of humor . . . He was mean, he was sadistic, he was masochistic, he resented everything.' But then she had ceased to love or to be faithful to him.

Elaine Scott
'My Elaine is a wonderful girl. I can write with her sitting in the room with me and that's the best that can be said . . . It is the first peace I have had with a woman.' Elaine (left) divorced to marry John. 'You've made my life bright', he told her on his deathbed.

Movie masterpiece
'It's a real good picture. I didn't have anything to do with it. Maybe that's why. It might be one of the best films I ever saw.' East of Eden *was screened all over the world (right) and consolidated the international fame Steinbeck by this time enjoyed.*

the front line and under fire at Salerno, near Naples, he experienced the full horror of war, the nightmare memories of which depressed him for months after his return home.

Steinbeck's only children, Thom and John, were born in 1944 and 1946. He loved the idea of them and had a romantic notion of their merits, but in reality they interrupted his work and he was probably a less than perfect father, being impatient for them to grow up. Meanwhile, his marriage was under strain from fame, separation and the couple's homeless wartime existence.

COSMOPOLITAN WRITER

Although associated exclusively with California in his early career, Steinbeck emerged as a cosmopolitan figure after the War. He wrote about people, not Californians, he argued. 'Home is people. I have no "place" home'. In fact New York City ultimately became his geographical home, and his summer house in Sag Harbour, Long Island, satisfied his lifelong love of the ocean.

In 1946 he travelled to Scandinavia. 'John Steinbeck, all of Denmark is at your feet', proclaimed one Copenhagen newspaper. The following year, he and the photographer Robert Capa went on an assignment to Russia, where they received a more muted welcome. Returning to the United States, Steinbeck had to cope with the painful death of Ed Ricketts and Gwyn's request for a divorce.

She told him that she had not loved him for years, nor been faithful to him. Unfortunately, John had idolized Gwyn and was loath to abandon the marriage. 'I am a very good lover but a lousy husband', he later concluded, but only after acting

out a bitter revenge on womankind, gratifying a 'goat-like lust', and drinking himself into a stupor. He felt betrayed and resentful for the rest of his life, but he remained close to his sons.

The last two decades of his life saw Steinbeck change direction. He remained a public figure, but not a fashionable one. The public still admired him (and bought his books), but progressive literary critics scorned him as a sentimental reactionary. In one respect they were right; Steinbeck was a curiously sentimental man. In spite of the scientific detachment with which he regarded *homo sapiens* as a species, he valued human friendship above all else. He also remained uncorrupted by fame and unaltered, though not unhurt, by criticism.

During the 1950s Steinbeck turned increasingly to journalism, covering both national presidential conventions in 1956. One of his most rewarding

Vietnam crusade
Steinbeck astonished liberal Americans with his outspoken support of US policy in Vietnam (right). He lashed out at the anti-war 'Vietniks' – 'dirty clothes, dirty minds'. His admiration was for the common soldiers (who included his son). But he wrote to a friend, 'I know we cannot win . . . And it seems . . . the design is for us to sink deeper and deeper into it.' He did not live to see it end.

In defence of a friend
Arthur Miller the playwright (left) came up for trial in 1957 by the House Un-American Activities Committee. Steinbeck sprang to his defence, and attacked public patriotism bought at the expense of 'private morality'. Miller wrote later, 'John had a fantastic and marvelous, the best kind of romantic streak.' No-one else had dared to speak up for him.

friendships at this time was with the twice-defeated Democratic candidate, Adlai Stevenson. He later developed a close friendship with Lyndon Johnson and became a supporter of the President's policy in Vietnam, an involvement for which many liberal Americans never forgave him.

The Nobel Prize in 1962 was a bolt from the blue. Steinbeck, who had not even known that he was in the running, felt greatly honoured and spent days rewriting his brief acceptance speech. But he neither needed money nor wanted exposure.

Throughout these years Steinbeck found unfailing strength in his devoted third wife, Elaine, whom he had married in 1950. With 'the Faire Elayne' as he called her, he began his unashamedly romantic quest for the truth about King Arthur, a subject that had fascinated him since childhood. 'All my life has been aimed at one book and I haven't started it yet', he wrote to a friend in 1961.

He never did. On 20 December 1968, after some months of ill health, he died of heart failure. At the funeral in New York City Henry Fonda read excerpts from Tennyson and Robert Louis Stevenson. But John Steinbeck did not come to rest on the East Coast after all. Shortly after Christmas Elaine and Thom committed his ashes to the wind on a cliff above the Pacific Ocean.

MA JOAD

In the winter of 1937 floods washed 4000 migrant unemployed from their tents and hovels in Visalia, California. Steinbeck went there to write about it. 'The newspapers won't touch the stuff but they will under my byline . . . If I can sell the articles I'll use the proceeds for serum and such.' He returned for *Life* magazine with photographer Horace Bristol. The woman (right) was the inspiration for Ma Joad, strength of character and suffering written in her features.

Horace Bristol/LIFE MAGAZINE 6/5/39 © Time Inc./Colorific!

Bruno Barbey/Magnum

THE GRAPES OF WRATH

Written out of indignation, this is the story of a bitter harvest of self-knowledge and pride ripening in a climate of indifference, ruthless capitalism and casual inhumanity.

Steinbeck wrote *The Grapes of Wrath* after visiting the camps of migrant workers who had made their way from drought-stricken Oklahoma to find work in California. During the long rainy season in February 1938, Steinbeck saw thousands of people starving, and knew he had to speak out.

The struggles of the Joad family as they make their immense journey west is Steinbeck's literary testimony to the hardship and exploitation suffered by the dispossessed during the Depression. *The Grapes of Wrath* is an epic novel; moving and compassionate, it tells a timeless story of the struggle for survival.

GUIDE TO THE PLOT

The novel opens with a description of drought and dying cornfields. A thick dust whipped up by a windstorm has settled on everything. The people wait, wondering what to do. Meanwhile Tom Joad, just out of jail for killing a man, is making his way home. He meets Casy, an ex-preacher, and together they walk back to the Joads' place. They find both house and land deserted. The tenant farmers have been evicted by the landowners and many of them have packed up to move west. Tom discovers his family are staying with his uncle John and have bought an old truck for their journey.

The Joads and Casy set out on Highway 66 in their burned-out, overladen vehicle, with barely enough money to last the trip. Their precarious life on the road is fraught with tragedy, but has many moments of humour and comradeship. Before they reach California, both Grampa and Granma have died, while the eldest son decides to stay in Arizona. Physically and emotionally exhausted,

Leaving home
"This truck was the active thing, the living principle . . . the new hearth, the living centre."

Behind the tractor
"The land bore under iron, and under iron gradually died", raped by tractors (right).

Zeta

Ma Joad urges the rest of the family on across the desert to the promised land. They soon have to face up to the scarcity of work and are forced to stay in squatter camps – invariably called Hooverville – on the outskirts of towns. All around them is rich and fertile land owned by a handful of businessmen interested only in maximizing their profits. The locals hate and despise the "Okies", cutting their wages and burning their camps at every opportunity.

TRUTH TO LIFE

The Joads are lucky enough to get a place at a well-organized government camp which is run on the basis of communal responsibility. Kindness and friendship – and washrooms – make the camp their best experience so far in California, but the lack of work means they must move on. They stop for a few days at the Hooper ranch to pick peaches in place of pickers who are on strike. But the rate is halved as soon as the strike is smashed, and they move on again.

Tom's quick temper again lands him in trouble with the law, and he is forced to live as a fugitive. But his anger develops into righteous indignation that encompasses the troubles of people beyond his own immediate family.

In defence of the controversial end of *The Grapes of Wrath*, Steinbeck wrote to a friend in 1939: 'I tried to write this book the way lives are being lived not the way books are written.' The novel is a slice of realism in fictional form, written to expose the plight of people like the Joads who fall victim to greedy landowners.

John Steuart Curry: *Baptism in Kansas* (1928). Oil on canvas. 40 × 50". Collection of Whitney Museum of American Art. Gift of Gertrude Vanderbilt Whitney. 31-159

Saving the People
Hellfire baptist preaching (above) is depicted as cowing the poor, "that all men might grovel and whine on the ground."

When the book was first published it attracted enormous attention, not least from the big farmers who accused Steinbeck of lies, misrepresentation, and even of being a communist. Steinbeck hated the 'hysteria', and did not accept that he

"They's stuff goin' on that the folks doin' it don't know nothin' about – yet. They's gonna come somepin outa all these folks goin' wes' – out all their farms lef' lonely. They's gonna come a thing that's gonna change the whole country."

Pat Fogarty

had written a subversive novel. The message to his readership was clear, however. Tom Joad, the central character, wonders why it isn't possible to "All work together for our own thing – all farm our own lan'." Steinbeck's simple answer was that the growers and their financiers would rather see everyone starve.

The unusual structure of the novel alternates descriptive and narrative chapters. It opens with a general description of the Dust Bowl and moves on to Tom's journey in the truck, breaking off to describe a land turtle's tremendous struggle to continue its own journey. The movements of the Joad family are given a wider perspective by the short, intervening chapters of commentary and general description. It is in these 'perspective' chapters that Steinbeck's voice comes through most directly. Like a great 19th-century novelist, he is unafraid to make direct comment about his characters and the society in which they live.

VIVID DIALOGUE

One of Steinbeck's greatest triumphs as a writer is his ability to write vivid dialogue, making the characters in *The Grapes of Wrath* spring to life. Their language is potent and earthy, and brings an emphatic realism to the text. Most of the novel is written in 'Okie' vernacular, in which humour plays a large part – sexual humour in particular. The style and struc-

ture underline the main concerns of the novel. The humour and deliberate repetition of language echo the unfailing desire of the human spirit to survive.

Casy, a preacher turned philosopher, is very much the mouthpiece for Steinbeck's views on the importance of the relationship between human beings and the natural world. Casy decides the best thing he can do with his life is to stay close to the earth and learn from the natural

rhythms of human existence: "Gonna learn why the folks walks in the grass, gonna hear 'em talk, gonna hear 'em sing . . . Gonna eat with 'em and learn."

The novel is rich in images drawn from the natural world to define the state of humans and comment on their behaviour. Highway 66, the route west, is described in relation to the land it crosses: "66 – the long concrete path across the country, waving gently up and down on the map . . . 66 is the path of a people in flight, refugees from dust and shrinking land . . . from the desert's slow northward invasion . . ."

People's connection with the land is a central theme of the novel. The Joad family and countless others like them have lived as tenant farmers for generations on the poor land around Sallisaw, working it as best they can, living close to nature, close to poverty. With the drought, the 'profit margin' of the landowners can no longer sustain the tenants and the community is smashed.

Muley Graves refuses to leave his home and wanders "around' like a ol' graveyard ghos'", keeping out of sight of the men who have come to clear the farms. Impassioned, he asks Casy and Tom how the landowners could be so heartless: " . . . them sons-a-bitches at their desks, they jus' chopped folks in two for their margin of profit. They jus' cut 'em in two. Place where folks live is them folks. They ain't whole, out

Hoe-down
There is a cynically orchestrated attempt to cause trouble at the migrant camp by infiltrators among the dancers (above).

A quick buck
"Cars limping along 66 like wounded things, panting and struggling." The garage owners (left) wait like vultures to prey on the cars' owners.

Telling secrets
Between them, the migrant children (right) – "wild . . . like animals" – work out their own social code of conduct. But Ruthie cannot keep a secret . . .

lonely on the road in a piled-up car. They ain't alive no more."

The further ordinary people get away from the land, the more the system breaks down. Utility farming with its huge acreage and machinery brings a death to the land: "Behind the tractor rolled the shining disks, cutting the earth with blades – not ploughing but surgery . . . the harrows combing with iron teeth . . ."

In the ascendancy are the used car sales-men, trading unroadworthy vehicles for dollars earned by real sweat and toil. The farming practised by the combines in California is a sin against nature and humanity. The rotting fruit, the wasted potatoes and the slaughtered pigs which people are not allowed near "is a crime . . . that goes beyond denunciation".

"Easy," she said. "You got to have patience. Why, Tom – us people will go on livin' when all them people is gone. Why, Tom, we're the people that live. They ain't gonna wipe us out. Why we're the people – we go on."

"We take a beatin' all the time." "I know," Ma chuckled . . . "But, Tom, we keep a-comin'."

"TO TOM WHO LIVED IT"

John Steinbeck's intimate knowl-edge of the dust-bowl migrants was thanks largely to a remarkable man called Tom Collins. Tom worked for the government Resettle-ment Administration (promoted right), managing camps which housed thousands of destitute 'Okies'. A patient, compassionate man, he believed a little food, shelter and respect could restore the dignity of these despised outcasts. As man-ager of Weedpatch Camp, he com-piled reports and collected songs and anecdotes in accurate dialect. Stein-beck, writing for the *San Francisco News* in 1936, seized avidly on this raw material and used it when he came to write *The Grapes of Wrath*. He acknowledged his debt with the novel's dedication.

Shahn, Ben. Years of Dust. 1937. Lithograph. 38 × 24¾". Collection. The Museum of Modern Art, New York. Gift of the designer.

Casy's years as a preacher and a wan-derer have made him uninterested in his own safety. He realizes the only way that the Joads and the hundreds of thousands of other migrants will survive is if they organize themselves as a working force. He inspires Tom with his ideas and there is a sense that no matter how dangerous the option, workers will organize, strikes will take place. In this way, some future for the Okies may be guaranteed.

HARDSHIPS AND PRIVATIONS

On a more immediate level, the Joads are able to survive the hardships and priva-tions they face because of their generosity of spirit. They even manage to show kindness to other folk worse off than themselves. Ma Joad has a theory that the hard times are simply a part of human existence and that people will survive, no matter how hopeless the future appears:
"Ever'thing we do – seems to me is aimed right at goin' on. Seems that way to me. Even get-tin' hungry – even bein' sick; some die, but the rest is tougher."

She is the backbone of the family, and is fierce in her determination to keep the family together: "She seemed to know that if she swayed the family shook, and if she ever really deeply wavered or despaired the family would fall . . ."

Her toughness and acceptance of hardship is rooted in her experience as a woman. She believes men find it difficult to adapt to change, but for "Woman, it's all one flow, like a stream, little eddies, little waterfalls, but the river, it goes right

Peter Newark's Western Americana

"Always some kind of crop to work in"
All the 'Okies' ask is the dignity of a job to do (above).

on." She takes it one day at a time, know-ing the most important thing is to feed everyone and keep the family together. She takes over from Pa in the decision-making, organizing their camp so that everyone's needs can be met. She voices the sentiment that underpins the novel:
"I'm learnin' one thing good . . . Learnin' it all a time, ever' day. If you're in trouble or hurt or need – go to poor people. They're the only ones that'll help – the only ones."

CHARACTERS IN FOCUS

The great strength of this novel lies in Steinbeck's portraiture. His sharp language and his quality of compassion produce the striking realism of Ma, Tom and Casy. They are unforgettable, both in themselves and in the concepts they represent. He invests them with a dignity that lifts them out of the degraded popular image of the time, insisting that they be credited with the heroism of martyrs.

WHO'S WHO

Ma Joad — The heart of the family; her determination to survive sustains everyone else.

Pa Joad — From the day his house is bulldozed, Pa "ain't been the same". Dispossessed, bewildered and uncertain, he relies heavily on his wife and sons.

Grampa and Granma — Grampa's childlike ways keep everyone amused. He and Granma – "as mean as her husband" – begin the long trek reluctantly, truculently.

Casy — Humane, pensive and humble, this former preacher travels with the Joads. Popular and charismatic, he finds a role as strike leader.

Tom Joad — Not even prison has destroyed Tom's tolerance and sense of responsibility. He is Ma's favourite son.

Rose of Sharon — Impressionable and self-centred, the daughter 'Rosasharn' is wholly bound up in her pregnancy.

Ruthie and Winfield — The "young fellas" of the family, whose future depends on the epic journey west.

Al Joad — The third son, with an invaluable knowledge of car engines which prompts Grampa to tell him, "You've growed up good."

Jim Rawley — Manager of the government camp and sympathetic to the migrants.

Connie — Rosasharn's adored 19-year-old husband.

Tom Joad (right) *has killed twice* in anger and maintains he would do the same again. But beneath a tough exterior, and in spite of the hard blows dealt him and his people, he is soft and idealistic. His mother believes him destined for greatness. As he grows in wisdom under the influence of Casy – a Christ-like figure – he too takes on a super-human universality. When events conspire to drive him away into the wilderness, he comforts his family by saying, "I'll be ever'where – wherever you look. Wherever they's a fight so hungry people can eat, I'll be there. Wherever they's a cop beatin' up a guy, I'll be there."

Ma Joad (left) *is the embodiment of Steinbeck's faith in the human spirit.* "Her hazel eyes seem to have experienced all possible tragedy and to have mounted pain and suffering like steps into a high calm and a super-human understanding." By contrast with her, *Pa Joad is a shadowy figure*, deprived of work and thus of his identity. He is a casualty of land-clearance, confused and lost. "I ain't no good any more. Spen' all my time a-thinkin' how it use' ta be".

The blind obstinacy of old age is personified in Grampa and Granma Joad (below). The spirit of life is strong in them – Granma with her hallelujahs and Grampa with his swearing. But they are too old to be uprooted from the lives and land they have called their own. "Vicious and cruel and impatient, like a frantic child", Grampa has a cantankerous, complaining, mischievous, laughing face. Granma "survived only because she was as mean as her husband. She had held her own with a shrill ferocious religiosity that was as lecherous and savage as anything Grampa could offer."

The real journey for Casy (right) **is one of self-discovery.** Once a preacher, he fell short of his faith in sleeping with the girls he preached to. Then his faith fell short of him, with its detachment from the real world of suffering and brotherhood. "There ain't no sin and there ain't no virtue. There's just stuff people do. It's all part of the same thing. And some of the things folks do is nice, and some ain't nice, but that's as far as any man got a right to say." Nevertheless, his words often echo Christ's. Out of passionate love of humanity he takes up the cause of the migrant workers.

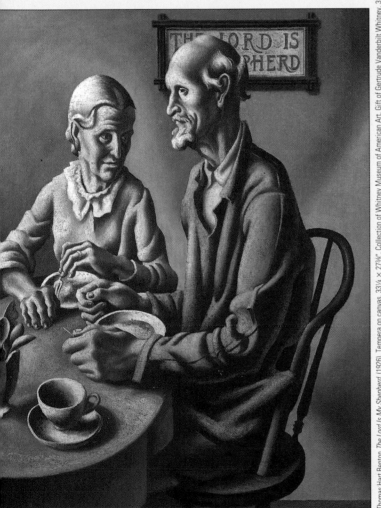

Vain and self-pitying, Rose of Sharon (right) **has much to learn about life's tragedies.** Under the careful, sometimes harsh protection of Ma, she is obliged to grow up as the family's situation worsens. 'Rosasharn' spends much of her time in an imaginary world of how things might be – or might have been. Her pregnancy also adds to the images of ripening which permeate the book: blighted fertility, wasted fecundity, the swelling grapes of wrath – all these recurring themes are borne along by Rose of Sharon towards an uncertain harvest, an overshadowed fruition.

'NATURAL SAINTS'

**Living and working among California's dispossessed,
Steinbeck revered their grandeur of spirit. To him they were
no blight on the landscape but the nation's 'natural saints'.**

In a letter to a friend about his novel *In Dubious Battle* (1936), John Steinbeck claimed that he was 'not interested in ranting about justice and oppression'. Rather, he had 'used a small strike in an orchard valley as the symbol of man's eternal, bitter warfare with himself'.

Steinbeck was probably exaggerating, since his books do show an unmistakable sympathy with the poor and helpless. By 1938 he was personally and financially involved in efforts to help thousands of migrant workers in California, when floods aggravated the starvation and sickness from which they were already suffering. But his statement does help to make it clear that, as a writer, he was not a committed social realist, let alone a political partisan. Moved to indignation by the plight of the migrant workers, he wrote a 60,000 word novel about their mistreatment – and straightaway scrapped it rather than publish a work of pure propaganda.

Only then did he settle down to produce *The Grapes of Wrath*. Both *In Dubious Battle* and *The Grapes of Wrath* – Steinbeck's supposedly 'proletarian' novels – are often far from flattering in their portraits of working people. These books therefore failed to please the politically orthodox of either Right or Left. His work caused similar offence in some quarters during World War II, when his novel about a Nazi-occupied country, *The Moon is Down* (1942), failed to present the situation in terms of absolute good versus absolute evil.

IN PRAISE OF HEROES

Despite the accuracy of his observation, Steinbeck was not a realist in the sense of being content to describe the ordinary course of life. Although most of his characters are 'ordinary' people, the ones that interest him are the heroic figures – figures such as Ma Joad and Casy in *The Grapes of Wrath,* or George in *Of Mice and Men,* who takes responsibility for Lennie's life and death. 'George is a hero and only heroes are worth writing about.' However great the odds, Steinbeck's most sympathetic characters strive with all their might to survive, and even dominate their circumstances.

This helps to explain the apparently disparate quality of Steinbeck's work, which included the 'proletarian' novels, the parable-like *The Pearl* (1947), the turbulent family saga *East of Eden* (1952) and humorous fantasies such as *Tortilla Flat* (1935) and *Cannery Row* (1945). Even the idle *paisanos* of *Tortilla Flat* are heroic:

Salinas Valley
*Steinbeck's
Californian roots
(below) shaped and
nurtured him.
Landscapes were
symbolic reference
points in his books,
often juxtaposing the
irony of human
suffering and
Nature's inalienable
beauty.*

Honest labourer
*(right) 'A couple of
years ago I realized
that I was not the
material of which
great artists are made',
wrote Steinbeck.
'. . . And since then
I have been happier
simply to do the
work and take the
reward . . . for a day
of honest work.'*

Spectrum Colour Library

effective devices, giving his work extra resonance and suggesting deeper levels of meaning.

As well as Arthurian lore, he drew on the Bible, the legend of Faust, Shakespeare's plays, and even (for *The Pearl*) the myths of the vanished Mayan civilization of Central America. Sometimes, as in the Cain and Abel theme of *East of Eden,* the parallel is very obvious, but more often Steinbeck uses such material unobtrusively. Not all readers will catch the resemblances in *The Grapes of Wrath* between the Okies' migration and the biblical exodus in search of the Promised Land, or notice those elements in *The Wayward Bus* (1947) that give the modern tale of a bus trip the momentous quality of a medieval pilgrimage. In the early stages of planning this book, Steinbeck made the significant remark that 'Juan Chicoy the driver is all the god the fathers you ever saw driving a six cylinder, broken down, battered world through time and space'.

Steinbeck was in fact a deeply serious artist whose apparent directness masked complex intentions – even *Cannery Row* was 'written on four levels'. Striving to master styles ranging from the flatly realistic to the sonorously biblical, he found writing hard, lonely work: 'I do not write easily. Three hours of writing require twenty hours of preparation.' It was fun when he found 'words crowding up to come tumbling out', but he was often 'near collapse' and a typical line from his letters is 'I have been doing a great deal of work, most of it no good and most of it thrown away.'

One result of this exhausting struggle was Steinbeck's relatively small output – only 18 volumes of fiction published over

"Danny's house was not unlike the Round Table, and Danny's friends were not unlike the knights of it" – a comparison kept up by means of mock-Arthurian chapter-headings. Although used light-heartedly in this instance, the incorporation of mythical and religious elements in his narratives was one of Steinbeck's most

Sea fever
Monterey (above) instilled in Steinbeck a lifelong love of the sea and life at the waterfront.

Dignity of labour
Spokesman for the underdog, Steinbeck lived and worked among Monterey's migrant workers (below). He championed the dignity and heroism of the ordinary labouring man (left) in the face of daily hardships.

William Gropper: Construction of the Dam. U.S. Department of the Interior, Washington/Brooks Photographers

The Pat Hathaway Collection of California Views

40 years. In his later years he experienced several creative crises and was haunted by the feeling that 'my time is over and I should bow out'. Although he came to believe that *East of Eden* represented his very best work, most readers find this and other later novels less powerful than his books of the 1930s.

HEADING EAST

Steinbeck's divorce and his move from California to New York in the early 1940s may have contributed to a decline in his talent, taking him away from the environment in which he had spent most of his life and found most stimulation – the memory-filled places such as the Salinas Valley and Monterey provided the settings for all his best fiction. California is as important in John Steinbeck's work as 'Wessex' in Thomas Hardy's.

Through his friendship with the marine biologist Ed Ricketts, Steinbeck gained his 'biological' view of life. His universe is conceived of as a single organism in which all the parts are interrelated. Both Ricketts and Steinbeck felt a reverence for life in all its forms. But, significantly, whereas Ricketts concluded that it was

wrong to interfere with natural processes, Steinbeck's outlook remained much more optimistic and active. With its message of hope and struggle, *The Grapes of Wrath* is still the most moving exposition of his ideas. Ma Joad comes at last to see that

Highest honours
Steinbeck was awarded the Nobel Prize as 'a teacher of goodwill and charity, a defender of human values' (right). He went in person to receive it despite being already a sick man.

Deepest misery
Although he recorded the utter despair and misery of the destitute (below), Steinbeck remained politically aloof and primarily concerned with his writing.

'the fambly' is not all that matters, and Casy glimpses – and acts on – the revelation that 'Maybe all men got one big soul ever'body's a part of.'

Steinbeck was a best-selling author – a fact that has obscured both his versatility and the long struggle he had for success. He began to attract attention only with his fourth book, *Tortilla Flat* (1935), a light-hearted fantasy calling into question the get-ahead American ethic. Steinbeck's social commitment inspired *Of Mice and Men* (1937), a brilliant short novel about unavoidable Fate, but it was the linked stories of *The Red Pony* (1937) which brought real, lasting fame. By contrast, the delightful *Cannery Row* (1945) is a retreat from the horrors of World War II into a Monterey never-never land of dead-beats, eccentrics and whores. In yet another vein, *The Wayward Bus* (1947) is an allegory of life's pilgrimage. Critics often detract from the later writings, but *East of Eden* (1952), a family saga, is one of his most popular books of all, and *Travels with Charley* (1962) has a uniquely easy-going, undidactic charm.

THE RED PONY
◆1937◆

Jody Tiflin is given his own pony to care for (right) in the first of four linked stories describing boyhood initiations into life and the conflict between childhood's heroic dreams and prosaic reality. Jody lives on a ranch in the Salinas Valley with his parents and the hired hand Billy Buck. In *The Gift*, Jody's failure to look after the pony leads to its death – and to the boy's first confrontation with the buzzards. In *The Great Mountains*, the old *paisano* (Mexican American) Gitano returns to the farm to die. He is rejected by Jody's father, but with the help of Jody and Billy finally rides off to the mysterious Great Mountains to the west. Jody gets a second chance to have his own foal in *The Promise*, but its birth is a traumatic event which brings out all Billy Buck's true mettle. *The Leader of the People* introduces Jody's grandfather, who typifies the 'westering' spirit of an earlier generation. To Jody's father, the old man is a ridiculous figure, but Jody's more sensitive reaction bodes well for his future.

Republic/Kobal Collection

Fine Art Photographic Library

TORTILLA FLAT
◆1935◆

Clad in ragged jeans, Danny and his friends form a goodly fellowship (left). Steinbeck sees them as a latterday King Arthur and his court, in this mock-heroic tale of *paisanos* in Monterey, sublimely indifferent to the all-American lust for money and success.

Young Danny comes home from the War to find that he has inherited two houses. His friends occupy one, although they never manage to pay any rent, until carelessness causes it to burn down. And so Pilon, Pablo, Jesus Maria, Big Joe Portagee and the huge, simple-minded Pirate (plus five dogs) move in with Danny. In their cobwebbed wooden home the friends lead the good life, loafing and philosophizing. In one entertaining episode after another their sharp wits and amiable lack of scruples keep them supplied with wine, food and women. Finally Danny enjoys a magnificent but tragic apotheosis at the greatest party ever seen in Tortilla Flat.

Cannery Row painting by Bruce Ariss © 1984 Monterey Bay Aquarium, photo by Geoffry Johnson

Warner Bros/Kobal Collection

CANNERY ROW
◆ 1945 ◆

That district of Monterey surrounding the sardine canneries (above) houses a rabble of free-spirits centring on the marine biologist Doc. Doc runs the Western Biological Laboratory, collecting specimens in the great tidal pool and living in his laboratory-home, where he listens to Bach and entertains a series of accommodating ladies. The other inhabitants of Cannery Row lead similarly rich lives: they include Mack and the boys of the Palace Flophouse and Grill, Dora and the girls of the Bear Flag whorehouse, Lee Chong the grocer, and Henri the avant-garde painter.

A sequel, *Sweet Thursday* (1954), describes how Mack and the boys set about providing Doc with a mate.

EAST OF EDEN
◆ 1952 ◆

Rivalry between brothers, first for their father's love and then for a woman (right), is the central theme of this ambitious novel. The biblical story of Cain and Abel is re-enacted over two generations by the Trasks – first by the half-brothers Adam and Charles, later by Adam's twin sons Aron and Caleb. Favoured less than the fair, smugly 'good' Aron, the dark, clever Caleb discovers that their mother is not dead, but that she deserted the boys shortly after their birth and now runs a high-class brothel. Caleb tries at first to preserve Aron's romantic illusions. But when his efforts are spurned, Caleb undertakes a disastrous revenge.

OF MICE AND MEN
◆ 1937 ◆

The simple-minded Lennie loves to pet soft, vulnerable creatures, including women (above). His friend George struggles in vain to keep him out of the trouble which invariably results from the unintentionally destructive use of Lennie's great strength. The two drifting farm hands find work on a Californian farm where the boss's aggressive son Curley picks on Lennie, and Curley's bored, lonely wife encourages his attentions. When Lennie's eagerness to touch and cherish something beautiful and fragile is thwarted once more, the ghastly repercussions sink him in difficulties from which even George cannot save him.

THE WAYWARD BUS
◆ 1947 ◆

'It is a cosmic bus holding sparks and back firing into the milky way turning the corner of Betelguese without a hand signal', wrote Steinbeck as he contemplated writing 'the most ambitious thing' he had ever attempted (right). It is no coincidence that the Mexican driver of the Californian bus, Juan Chicoy, has the initials J.C. The story tells of a group of 'pilgrims', each making their hapless journey through life with different motives, different attitudes, but unwittingly to the same inescapable destination.

ONLY THE GREAT

JOHN STEINBECK
could create
THE WAYWARD BUS
and its **runaway** people... **runaway** loves... **runaway** emotions!

"I married you because I couldn't keep my hands off you ..."

"Just because a girl's a blonde, guys think all you've got to do is—"

"Aren't you going to make a pass at me?"

STARRING
JOAN COLLINS · JAYNE MANSFIELD · DAN DAILEY
with RICK JASON and Betty Lou Keim
Dolores Michels · Larry Keating
from 20th CENTURY-FOX in
CinemaScope®
Produced by **CHARLES BRACKETT** · Directed by **VICTOR VICAS** · Screenplay by **IVAN MOFFAT**
Based on the Novel by John Steinbeck

TRAVELS WITH CHARLEY
◆ 1962 ◆

With no-one but his wife's poodle for company (left), John Steinbeck made a journey by truck through the United States so as to prove himself still independent from the routine of domesticity, to gain the different perspective of an itinerant and to discover, incognito, what had become of modern America. The result was *Travels with Charley*, a mixture of fiction and non-fiction, an outlet for his thoughts and philosophies and general good nature. Reviewers loved it, and it sold more on publication than any other Steinbeck book. Although specific to the time at which it was written, it has enough of the essential, mellow, wry Steinbeck of later years to make enjoyable reading today.

The Dust Bowl disaster was only one aspect of a national economic crisis which called into question the entire American ethic and polarized the haves and have-nots as never before.

The *Grapes of Wrath* caused a furore when it was published in 1939. In it, the author pronounced several American institutions to be enemies of a substantial segment of the American people. He accused bankers and financiers of heartless indifference to the victims of natural calamity. He indicted powerful landowners for dispossessing the afflicted and then cynically exploiting their desperation for work. His accusation was levelled, in fact, at the whole American economic structure, condemning the ethic of capitalism as a system of exploitation, veiled during the good times, but revealed in its naked ugliness when the bad times came. Private and corporate greed, Steinbeck implied, shreds the fabric of society and demeans rich and poor alike.

When the book first appeared, followed shortly by the film, Americans were stunned. The message was lacerating to a degree unprecedented in American literature. Naturally, those who found themselves vilified by Steinbeck spluttered that it was simply not true. Most Americans, however little they knew of Oklahoma, had a feeling in their bones that it was true. And tens of thousands who had, like the Joads, made that dispiriting trek from the Plains to the Pacific knew without a shadow of a doubt that he was right. It was their own tragic story.

WALL STREET CRASH

The Dust Bowl calamity on which the book is based was in fact a relatively small component of the bigger disaster known as the Great Depression. The 1920s were boom times for the United States, and the prosperity was reflected in share prices on the New York stock exchange, which rose to dizzying heights by the summer of 1929. Then, in the autumn of that year, the market fell sharply, rallied briefly, then slumped.

The Wall Street Crash had a dire and lasting effect on the American economy. Investments and savings were wiped out, businesses went bankrupt, and banks themselves went broke daily. The old values of thrift and financial prudence suddenly made no sense. Unemployment soared to reach 14 million in early 1933 – more than a quarter of the workforce.

There had been financial panics and economic depressions before (as recently as the 1890s), but the overall trend, from earliest colonial times, had been towards increasing prosperity. On a psychological level, the Great Depression was a shattering experience, much more so for Americans than for Europeans undergoing a similar slump. The American Dream presupposed economic well-being and the opportunity to work hard for tangible rewards. Suddenly, millions of people who had, during the 1920s, attained the highest standard of living in the history of the world fell into poverty. Furthermore, there was no safety net between them and destitution.

Charitable organizations such as the YMCA and the Salvation Army did what they could to alleviate the suffering. They set up breadlines and soup kitchens which soon became familiar sights in cities from coast to coast.

During 1930 and 1931, the Depression deepened. President Herbert Hoover, in many ways an able, intelligent man, seemed not to grasp the magnitude of the disaster. Recovery, he tried to reassure his fellow citizens, was 'just around the corner'. In fact, the worst was yet to come. The stock market continued to slide, and manufactur-

Dust to dust
The thriving fertility of the southern wheat fields (below) was swallowed up, in the space of 50 years, by an ocean of dust (above). A massive, man-made ecological disaster drove 60 per cent of the population away in search of a livelihood and contributed to the country's economic plight.

Appeals to the President and persistent lobbying of Congress proved fruitless, but thousands of BEF members were unwilling to take 'no' for an answer. They camped out in Washington in tents and shanties and deserted buildings, and resisted all attempts by the authorities to persuade them to leave the capital and go home.

Summer wore on and then, in late July, the uneasy peace was broken. During a minor scuffle, the police panicked and shot dead two veterans. The army was called in, with General Douglas MacArthur in command (and Major Dwight D. Eisenhower as his aide). MacArthur ignored Hoover's order not to attack the demonstrators. His army moved into the shanty town in force, complete with teargas and swords. While no-one was killed, scores of veterans were injured, and the BEF was driven out of the capital. MacArthur would have the opportunity to bury this shabby

ing output to fall. Unemployment rose inexorably. By the summer of 1932 the nation's mood was one of sullen bitterness, and Hoover was held to blame.

His bungled handling of what was known as the 'Bonus Army' confirmed the harsh judgement of him as a heartless president. Starting off in Portland, Oregon, some 300 jobless veterans of World War I set off for Washington DC. Their intention was to demand advance payment of a bonus Congress had granted veterans in 1924 but scheduled for settlement in 1945. As they neared the capital in truck convoy, their numbers swelled as more and more unemployed veterans – some with their families – joined this self-styled Bonus Expeditionary Force. By the time it reached Washington at the end of May it numbered 20,000.

Wall Street Crash
Fortunes were lost overnight (left) as the inflated value of shares on the stock market plummeted.

Bonus Army rout
Shameful scenes (above) of troops scattering demonstrating war veterans badly discredited the government.

Small-town ruin
The loss of public confidence in investment saw banks go bankrupt in small towns throughout the nation (right).

incident beneath heroic achievements in World War II; but Hoover's reputation was wrecked. The disillusioned BEF left this bitter parody as their epitaph:

> Hoover is our shepherd;
> We are in want.
> He maketh us to lie down on the park benches;
> He leadeth us beside the still factories;
> He disturbeth our soul.
> He leadeth us in the path of destruction for his party's sake.
> Yea, though we walk through the valley of the Depression,
> We anticipate no recovery for those who art with us.
> The politicians and diplomats frighten us.
> Thou preparest a reduction of our salary in the presence of our enemies;
> Our expenses runneth over.
> Surely poverty and unemployment will follow us
> Through all the days of the Republican administration
> And we will dwell in mortgaged homes forever.

As 1932 wore on, it was obvious that this slump was not like its predecessors, not the sort of tem-

A new dealer
The fall from grace of Herbert Hoover helped Franklin D. Roosevelt to power (the two are pictured right at the Inauguration). Roosevelt promised a 'New Deal', but what he primarily delivered was a new spirit of optimism after years of self-defeating despair.

On the breadline
Soup kitchens (below) and breadlines meant the difference between life and death for the destitute unemployed of the cities. At first the relief was provided by charities; later the State took over and footed the bill.

porary downturn that could be accepted as part of the economic cycle. The nation was in serious trouble, and there was a fear that the whole social and economic infrastructure might collapse under the strain. The Bolshevik Revolution in Russia was a fairly recent event, while the rise of various fascist movements in Europe was about to culminate in Hitler's Third Reich.

It was against this backdrop that the 1932 presidential election was contested. The American

Louis hidak *Home Relief Station.* (1935-6). Oil on canvas. *28 × 36".* Collection of Whitney Museum of American Art. Purchase. 36.148

Swiftly abandoning his election promises to balance the budget, Roosevelt accepted the need to spend what it took to provide relief, something he saw as the necessary precondition for genuine recovery. The Federal Emergency Relief Administration was set up to grant relief funds to the individual states for distribution as 'dole'. Another relief measure was the Civilian Conservation Corps, which aimed to get young unemployed men out of the labour market and into camps where they could be gainfully employed on various conservation and construction projects. During its eight-year existence, the CCC attracted some three million young people who worked on wide ranging projects such as road-building and flood control.

The CCC was just one of a host of new governmental bodies known as the 'alphabet

voters turned to Franklin D. Roosevelt, the governor of New York. Roosevelt was a wealthy, upper-class career politician, widely viewed in political circles as a charming, indolent lightweight – a dilettante. He certainly had no reputation for intellect.

It is likely that the electorate voted Hoover out rather than Roosevelt in, because Roosevelt's campaign promises of a 'New Deal' for the American people were couched in vague, frequently contradictory generalities. Certainly no-one could have anticipated the new President's activity when he assumed office on 4 March 1933.

FIRESIDE CHATS

Roosevelt immediately declared a nationwide bank holiday for the following day, then rammed emergency banking legislation through a special session of Congress. On Sunday 12 March, he went on radio to explain the new policy which was aimed at stopping further bank closures. Government agencies were to investigate each bank's solvency. Those that were deemed sound would be allowed to re-open; those that were not would stay shut.

This broadcast was the first of Roosevelt's 'fireside chats'. These talks were to become a feature of his long years in office. In his inaugural address he had stated his belief that 'the only thing we have to fear is fear itself'. The fireside chats were his way of allaying that fear. Reassurance on its own would have been empty rhetoric, but Roosevelt confounded his detractors by the speed and scope of his action. The latent powers of the American president are immense: Roosevelt simply began to use them in a way no-one had done before. During his first, famous 'Hundred Days', Congress passed a phenomenal quantity of new legislation.

Home Relief
One of the Home Relief stations (above) set up by President Roosevelt's New Deal administration.

'Alphabet' aid
Field offices of the WPA (right) directed the unemployed towards work; the NRA (inset) injected aid to industry.

'Labour' camps
Federal funds built vast communities like the one below near Washington – places to live and work with dignity.

Peter Newark's Western Americana

Library of Congress/Macdonald/Aldus Archive

75

GOLD DIGGERS of 1935

agencies' such as the Civil Works Administration (CWA), which provided relief work for several million people – including artists paid to provide paintings in public places; the National Recovery Administration (NRA), which was set up to stimulate and control industrial production; and the Tennessee Valley Authority (TVA), which was an immensely ambitious scheme to harness the mighty Tennessee River and provide hydro-electric power.

A RAY OF HOPE

The New Deal represented a massive extension of government activities in areas previously considered private domain. But it remains debatable how far legislation was responsible for dragging the United States out of the Depression. It would require the advent of World War II fully to revive the American economy. The New Deal can at best be described as having contributed to recovery. But Roosevelt's sunny personality, his strong, mellifluous voice and his implacable determination to do something – anything – to get the stricken nation back on its feet made a major contribution to national morale. Those suffering the worst hardships at least came to believe that the most powerful man in the land genuinely cared about their plight and was trying to alleviate it.

No amount of compassion or innovation, however, could avert the Dust Bowl tragedy, which struck during the early years of the Roosevelt administration. The Southern Plains of the Texas panhandle, Oklahoma and the adjacent areas of Kansas, Colorado and New Mexico form a natural bowl. A strong wind originating in the Gulf of Mexico blows steadily through this bowl. There is little rainfall and no trees. Tough prairie grass is all that holds the soil in place and preserves the moisture to nourish it. During the latter half of the 19th century, the delicate balance of nature was seriously disrupted by overgrazing. Dust and snow storms were the result. Then, in the early 20th century, cattle farming gave way to wheat growing. This was a recklessly short-sighted move, because it meant breaking the soil and destroying the precious grass which held the topsoil in place.

When the price of wheat fell sharply with the

Escapism
In reaction to all the drab, unrelenting poverty and the possible crack-up of the social fabric, the entertainment industry produced hugely lavish, glamorous shows and films (left). The public were invited to wallow in opulence and frivolous unreality. Arguably it was the safety valve which relieved an otherwise intolerable pressure.

'Struggle to find work'
Photographer Horace Bristol was on assignment with Steinbeck in California when he took the photograph below of men competing for work.

onset of the Depression, the farmers could only respond by growing more wheat. This was virtually suicidal. They saw their farms simply blown away in 'black blizzards'. Dust swallowed up homesteads, lives, landscapes, and there was no crop to harvest. Tenant farmers and farm labourers were an expensive luxury rendered unnecessary by shiny new tractors drawing the last life out of the soil.

The flight from the Dust Bowl became a mass exodus. Some counties lost 60 per cent of their population – most families, like the Joads, packed up their belongings and trekked west – migrant workers seizing on any chance to pick fruit or cotton or work as unskilled labourers. The wage for such workers was driven down and down as the competition for jobs grew ever greater. *The Grapes of Wrath* is an indictment of a social system which placed the profit motive above the true wealth of the country – its people. It is also a tribute to the nobility of the human spirit that such qualities as decency, compassion and generosity were actually able to survive the blight of those years of poverty and deprivation.

ERNEST HEMMINGWAY

✦ *1899-1961* ✦

The excitement of Hemingway's novels was equalled by his
action-packed life – a life spattered with the blood of war,
hunting, bullfights and brawls. His heroes overcome disaster
through a combination of idealism, strength and courage. But
Hemingway was driven from one adventure to the next, from
one woman's bed to another's – and finally to suicide – by a
burning need to excel. A need which extended also to his writing,
where he strove, with equal determination, for perfection.

"FRAID A NOTHING"

Bold and daring even as a child, Hemingway had a reputation within his family for being "fraid a nothing". And his determined bravado was not to be shaken by war, illness or personal tragedy.

Before he became a writer, Ernest Hemingway was a fisherman, a boxer, a lover of blood sports and a war hero. This raw experience of life enabled him to write with a passion and intensity that set him apart from other writers, and transformed the man into a legend.

Hemingway was born on 21 July 1899 in Oak Park, Illinois, a prosperous suburb of Chicago. Hemingway's father, Dr Clarence (Ed) Hemingway, was a big, strong man, who passed on to his son a passion for hunting, fishing and a pioneer existence. His mother Grace was, in contrast, a sensitive and religious woman. She sang in the local choir and named her daughters after the saints. She was keen for Ernest, the second of her six children, to study music, and to that end she bought him a cello. But his father gave him a fishing rod at three, and a gun at ten. His influence prevailed until tragedy struck much later.

A COWARD'S WAY OUT

In 1928, troubled by financial worries and the state of his health, Ed Hemingway shot and killed himself. His son, nearing 30, was devastated. As he was to write in *For Whom the Bell Tolls,* "I'll never forget how sick it made me the first time I knew he was a *cobarde* . . . Coward." He felt disgraced by his father's suicide, sullied and diminished by such an ignoble end. In one action of a Civil War revolver, both father and a boy's image of idealized manhood had died.

Hemingway's childhood was unexceptional. At two he reputedly used to shout that he was "fraid a nothing". He grew up with four sisters, wishing that he had a brother with whom to share manly exploits. Twice he ran away from home, but never for long. He was a good student, read voraciously and had his first short story published in the school magazine in his final year, 1916-17.

After he graduated from high school, Hemingway wanted to start living. He had no time for university, and instead joined the *Kansas City Star* as a junior reporter. He worked on the paper for seven months, honing his style and his art, but with the outbreak of World War I in Europe, he longed to shed his mid-western cocoon and join the action. He volunteered twice but was rejected because of weak sight.

In 1918, he heard that the Red Cross needed volunteers for the Italian Army and decided that this was his opening. He was selected, and, in the uniform of an honorary second lieutenant, was transported across France to Milan. The war was raging, and on the very first day the teenage Hemingway had a sudden and dramatic initiation into manhood. A munitions factory had exploded, and along with other ambulancemen Hemingway had to pick up what was left of dozens of mutilated bodies, many of them women. On the Front, shells were falling like rain. A man was injured, Hemingway tried to carry him to safety and was caught in machine-gun fire himself. With over 200 fragments of metal in his legs and body, he lost consciousness. 'I blacked out. I wanted to

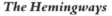

The Hemingways
Ernest is seated between his sisters Ursula (left) and Marcelline, and his redoubtable parents. He felt betrayed years later by his father's sudden suicide.

Mid-western boyhood
Growing up in Illinois (above and right) gave Ernest many outdoor pleasures. Later he was to hunt and fish with his wives, and teach his sons the skills he had learnt from his father.

run but couldn't, like those nightmares everyone has had.'

Hemingway was admitted to the American Red Cross Hospital in Milan, where, in the course of twelve operations, the doctors managed to save his legs. For his bravery at the Front, the Italians awarded him a silver medal for valour.

A by-product of his hospital stay was that Hemingway fell deeply in love. The woman was a nursing sister, Agnes Hannah von Kurowsky, a tall, slim beauty from Washington DC. When he was sent back to the States he wrote to her every day, but she was ten years his senior and loath to become involved with a man not yet 20. As with many of the most powerful experiences in his life, Hemingway was to draw on it later, describing a passionate love between a wounded soldier and a nurse in *A Farewell to Arms.*

DREAMS OF EUROPE

Recovered in body though still badly shaken, Hemingway returned to Oak Park, Illinois, where he dreamed of Agnes, of Europe, and of a world more dazzling than his provincial home. He suffered from insomnia and nightmares. In an attempt to purge his war memories, he wrote about them, but his thoughts remained in Europe. Relations with his mother – never good – were worsening. Restless, he moved to Chicago, where, in the autumn of 1920, he met the woman who was to become the first Mrs Hemingway.

Eight years his senior, Elizabeth Hadley Richardson was an accomplished pianist, tall and graceful, much impressed by the wit and world-liness of the handsome war hero. They married in

V.A. Serov - Landscape with Overgrown Pond/Bridgeman Art Library

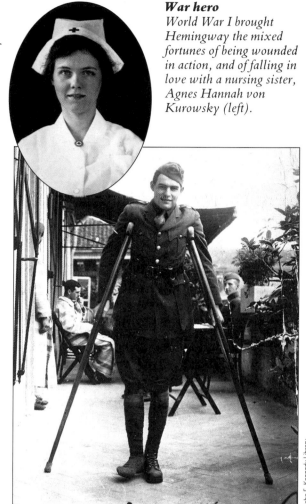

War hero
World War I brought Hemingway the mixed fortunes of being wounded in action, and of falling in love with a nursing sister, Agnes Hannah von Kurowsky (left).

John F. Kennedy Library

Paris in the '20s
Hemingway's talents blossomed in Paris (right), where 'the very air was suffused with style'.

Key Dates

1899 born in Illinois

1918 joins Red Cross. Wounded in Italy

1921 marries Hadley Richardson

1926 *Fiesta*

1927 marries Pauline Pfeiffer.

1928 Father's suicide

1929 *A Farewell to Arms*

1937 Reports on Spanish Civil War

1940 *For Whom the Bell Tolls.* Marries Martha Gellhorn

1946 marries Mary Welsh

1953 Pulitzer Prize

1954 Nobel Prize

1961 commits suicide

Max Ludby: Notre Dame from the river/Fine Art Photographic Library

On safari
Hemingway was fascinated by the 'dark continent' and viewed it, like a giant bullfighting arena, as a place to test heroism. He first went hunting there in 1932 and returned 21 years later, once again to pit courage, manhood, and rifle against big game.

1921 and, on the advice of the novelist Sherwood Anderson, decided to head for Paris, where, according to Henry James, the very air was suffused with style.

Hemingway managed to secure a commission from the *Toronto Star* to write a series of Letters from Europe, and, armed with introductions to such avant-garde writers as Gertrude Stein and Ezra Pound, the couple sailed to Europe.

Paris proved the fertile ground that Hemingway had hoped, and he felt in his element there. He lived a bohemian life, frequenting boulevard cafés, having sparring matches with his new

John Hadley Nicanor
Named after a Spanish bullfighter, 'Bumby' (above) was to have only a couple of years of family life before his parents divorced.

The four Mrs Hemingway
From left to right, the women whom Hemingway married till death (or divorce) should part them were: Hadley Richardson (1921-27); Pauline Pfeiffer (1927-40); Martha Gellhorn (1940-45); Mary Welsh (1946-61).

which brought him little money. Gradually, however, his prospects began to brighten, although irrevocable damage had been done to his marriage. Over the next two years, *In Our Time, The Torrents of Spring* and *The Sun Also Rises (Fiesta)*, were published, the last of which was a commercial as well as critical success. James Joyce was later to say of him, 'He's a good writer, Hemingway. He writes as he is . . . He's a big, powerful peasant, as strong as a buffalo . . . And ready to live the life he writes about.'

SUCCESS AND REMARRIAGE

By now Hemingway was quite a celebrity, much sought after as man and writer. Newspapers and magazines wrote fulsomely about him. Paris *Vogue* sent their fashion editor, Pauline Pfeiffer, to interview him. The interview proved fruitful. Pauline was an intelligent, serious girl from a wealthy Catholic family. From the first, she set her sights on Hemingway. Hemingway was flattered, and captivated. He asked Hadley for a divorce. She insisted on a 100-day separation between Hemingway and Pauline. If he still wanted to marry after that, she would agree to divorce him.

Hadley duly stepped aside; but after the divorce Hemingway apparently wept like a child, called himself 'a son of a bitch' and felt that he had done Hadley, the perfect wife, a terrible wrong. To ease his conscience he arranged for the royalties from *The Sun Also Rises* to be paid to her. As he told his

friends, and enjoying the companionship and support of his fellow writers James Joyce, Ezra Pound, Wyndham Lewis and Gertrude Stein.

With Hadley, Hemingway travelled to Spain, and together they saw the bulls galloping through the streets of Pamplona in a yearly ritual of daring and showmanship. It was a spectacle that imprinted itself on Hemingway's mind, particularly because of the bravery of one of the matadors, Nicanor Villalta. By this time Hadley, to Hemingway's displeasure, had become pregnant. She wanted to have her child on home soil and this meant packing up and leaving Paris. In a drunken moment Hemingway confessed to Gertrude Stein, 'I am too young to be a father'. But a father he became on 10 October 1923, when John Hadley Nicanor was born, named after the Spanish bullfighter and later nicknamed 'Bumby'.

Wife and son were well, but Hemingway was finding the confines of Toronto stultifying. Within three months of Bumby's birth, the Hemingways returned to Paris, and to the squalor of a flat on the rue Notre Dame des Champs. Hemingway tried his hand at a number of jobs to earn some money, but times were hard. He stopped buying clothes, patched his old jackets, and allowed others to treat him. For Hadley, at home with her new baby, the reality was considerably bleaker.

Eventually, Hemingway helped edit the *Transatlantic Review*, a prestigious position but one

BULLFIGHTING

Throughout his life Hemingway was obsessed with concepts of honour, particularly courage in the face of death. To him, the *corrida* (bullfight) represented the ultimate test of a man. He had watched with awe those youths who raced and cavorted before wild bulls in the streets of Pamplona, marvelling at their ritual dance with death.

In *For Whom the Bell Tolls,* Hemingway often likens a character's courage – or lack of it – to that of a matador. Hemingway himself faced the bulls in the ring in Pamplona, and acquitted himself with honour. He later named his first son after a famous matador.

friend F. Scott Fitzgerald, 'Hadley has been grand and everything has been my fault in every way.'

On 10 May 1927 he and Pauline were married in a Catholic church in Paris. But the city was starting to lose its charms. Hemingway's thoughts turned to the wide open spaces of his native land, and in the following year he and Pauline returned to America and set up home in Key West, Florida.

America was the land of opportunity, and Hemingway, nearly 30, was determined to make the most of it. Gone were the days of eking out a meagre existence in Paris attics. He lived in style, bought a yacht, went fishing and drank to excess. Hemingway was becoming one of his own heroes – tough, battered, laconic.

AFRICAN ADVENTURE

With Pauline he had two more sons, Patrick and Gregory, but contentment eluded him. His father had by now committed suicide and Hemingway struggled with a growing sense of disillusionment. In search of adventure, he and Pauline set off on a hunting expedition to Africa, in the course of which he killed big game and stored up experiences for some of his best short stories, including 'The Snows of Kilimanjaro' and 'The Short Happy Life of Francis Macomber'.

More successes followed – novels, film rights, even greater fame – but they did not bring happiness. When the Spanish Civil War broke out in 1936, Hemingway, the lover of all things Spanish, had to be there. His sympathies lay with the Popular Front, against General Franco, and with a loan of $40,000 he bought a fleet of ambulances for the Loyalist army. He visited Madrid four times, reporting on all aspects of the conflict until the city fell in 1939. He felt young again – involved, in danger, needed.

Hemingway was, of course, not alone. Thousands had volunteered and it was these heroic men and women whom Hemingway immortalized in *For Whom the Bell Tolls*. Apart from his novel, another significant outcome of those years was the breakup of Hemingway's second marriage.

Before Hemingway had left for Spain, he had met Martha Gellhorn, a bright, politically astute journalist. Blonde and elegant, she had already had a novel and a book of short stories published. She was intriguing and Hemingway, already tiring of Pauline, wanted her. When Martha was later sent to Spain to cover the war, their relationship took off. In 1940, 'after four years of living in enjoyable sin' (as Martha put it), they were married, and Pauline and her sons were awarded the house in Key West.

The marriage gave Hemingway the chance to move again, to shed one life and start a new one. But on their honeymoon, Martha covered the war in China for *Collier's* magazine, and Hemingway found himself in the unaccustomed position of being an appendage to an awesomely independent woman. In many ways, the honeymoon was already over. On their return, Hemingway and

Beloved city
In 1948 Hemingway returned to Europe to revisit old haunts. Venice (above) opened her arms to the now famous war hero.

Martha moved to Cuba and set up home in the Finca Vigía, in Havana. Cuba, Hemingway felt, was closest in spirit to his beloved Spain, and here he settled to a life of luxury.

But in 1941, the Japanese attacked Pearl Harbor, and the United States were at war. Martha was once again sent to cover the war, and

Fact or Fiction

THE REAL MARIA

In the spring of 1938, during the Spanish Civil War, Hemingway visited a hospital north of Barcelona where he met a particularly gentle and devoted nurse. Hemingway learned that early in the conflict she had been captured and raped by fascist soldiers, and he retold her tragic story in the words of another Maria in *For Whom the Bell Tolls*.

In appearance, however, his Maria was fashioned as a private tribute to his third wife, Martha Gellhorn, with her blonde hair "like a wheatfield in the wind".

Cuban exile
After 20 years in Havana, Hemingway felt virtually Cuban; he admired Castro (above) but was alarmed by the implications of his takeover in 1959.

Hemingway was sent as a correspondent for the Royal Air Force, a commission set up by Roald Dahl, then Assistant Air Attaché to the British Embassy in Washington.

Separately, the two were sending off dispatches to *Collier's*: Hemingway's full of vitality but often grossly inaccurate, Martha's closer to the action and ever competent. Already a rift was appearing in their marriage. Hemingway wanted a daughter; Martha refused to have a child by him. And the similarity of interests which had initially drawn

them together was now a source of friction. They competed constantly – in their work, in their home life. Martha was as brave and as independent as the Hemingway hero, and Hemingway was fast becoming a shadow of his fictional ideal.

Although Hemingway was awarded a bronze medal for his part in the Normandy landings, it was more by accident than by design that he was there. Martha, certainly, was unimpressed. He said of her later that 'Martha was the biggest mistake' in a life full of mistakes.

WIFE NUMBER FOUR

A woman who clearly was not a mistake for Hemingway was Mary Welsh. He met Mary in war-torn London in 1944. She, too, was a journalist, small, blonde, from Minnesota. In 1946 he married her, his fourth and last wife – who he called 'Papa's Pocket Rubens'.

He was happy with her, but not with himself. He was tired. The effects of the last 40 hectic years were beginning to tell on his health. His eyesight had worsened and doctors were worried that he might become blind. Writing became difficult. Secretly he feared that he was a victim of his own maxim – 'We do not have great writers. Something happens to our good writers at a certain age.'

In 1953 Hemingway and Mary decided to go on a second safari to Africa. But this time it almost resulted in tragedy. They were involved in not one but two air crashes, and although Hemingway had twice more cheated death, the crashes had left indelible scars on his already troubled mind.

The writer's health was now deteriorating fast. Heavy drinking had damaged his liver, his blood pressure was too high and his doctors warned him to keep off fat, drink and women.

In the meantime the situation in Cuba had worsened. Hemingway feared that his adopted country might be plunged into a civil war, and anti-American feelings were running high. Hemingway knew little of Castro's politics and was worried that he and Mary might be deported.

DEFEATED HERO

In 1960 the Hemingways left Cuba and settled near Ketchum, Idaho, in a tranquil, isolated house on a windswept hillside. Hemingway was now a pathetic figure, frail, depressed and insecure. Several times he tried to kill himself but was prevented by Mary's loving vigilance. His doctors recommended a course of electric shock treatments and, after a spell in hospital, Hemingway returned home, seemingly improved.

But then on 2 July 1961, Hemingway rose early, loaded a double-barrelled shotgun and fired it into his mouth. The man who had boxed in Paris, skied in Austria, fished in Florida, hunted in Africa and fought in several wars had shot himself. He lay sprawled on the floor in his home, with his favourite hunting gun by his side. The writer who had lived by the gun had died by it. He was, after all, mortal.

A final retreat
Troubled by deteriorating health, and deeply depressed, Hemingway moved to an isolated hillside house near Ketchum, Idaho (right). Tragically, one morning, shotgun in hand, he took his life, just as his father had done.

FOR WHOM THE BELL TOLLS

Intertwining a love story with events in a civil war, Hemingway pays tribute to the heroism of ordinary people willing to lay down their lives for their beliefs.

Widely believed to be Hemingway's greatest novel, *For Whom the Bell Tolls* has been described as 'the best fictional report on the Spanish Civil War that we possess'. But it is far more than a historically accurate account of a war. It is about people, and their dreams and ideas; and it is a love story.

The novel presents the action through the eyes of a small guerrilla band hiding out in the mountains. Although the events span only three days, Hemingway ranges backwards and forwards in time, giving the story far wider horizons than its immediate confines of caves, pine forest and open sky. The small struggle of one ill-equipped band of fighters is symbolic of all struggles, and the story of a man trying to love a woman against insurmountable odds is the story of all ill-fated love affairs.

Engrossing, uplifting, and deeply tragic, *For Whom the Bell Tolls* is ultimately a tribute to the heroism of the ordinary people of Spain, who were forced to fight against the rising tide of fascism sweeping across their country at that time.

GUIDE TO THE PLOT

Robert Jordan, a young American college lecturer, joins one of the International Brigades to fight for the Republican cause in the Spanish Civil War. His enormous love for Spain and its people as well as his hatred for fascism have made him into an extremely fervent guerrilla. He has orders from the Russian General Golz to blow up a strategically important bridge behind fascist lines. It is a difficult operation for which he needs help. Anselmo, an old trustworthy guide, leads Jordan to Pablo's band of gypsies who are in hiding in the mountains.

Pablo is suspicious of Jordan and reluctant to be drawn into the fighting. He refuses to help the American blow up the bridge, partly because of the danger and partly because it will mean he and his camp will have to move on. But his woman, Pilar, pledges support for Jordan's plan and sets about organizing the band.

Among the group is Maria, a young woman, who has been brutally raped by fascist soldiers when they stormed her

Adrian Stokes: Twilight in a Forest. Private Collection/Bridgeman Art Library

Pine forest retreat
Rescued by Pablo's band from the fascists, Maria (right and below) is gradually recovering from the wounds inflicted on her. Fascist soldiers raped her, imprisoned her, shaved her head and murdered her parents before her eyes. Now, with the pine forests as her home and Pilar as her protectress, she is growing strong again.

A loyal band
Maria holds a special place among the gypsies (below), although Pilar guards her jealously. She is a part of them but belongs to no man — until, that is, she sets eyes on the 'Inglés', Robert Jordan (far right).

Kobal Collection

> *"Then there was the smell of heather crushed and the roughness of the bent stalks under her head and the sun bright on her closed eyes and all his life he would remember the curve of her throat with her head pushed back into the heather roots and her lips that moved smally and by themselves and the fluttering of the lashes on the eyes tight closed against the sun and against everything…"*

town. With the memory of her parents being shot before her eyes, Maria is one of the many orphaned victims of the war. She has survived largely due to the efforts of Pilar, who looks after her with a love both fierce and tender.

When Jordan sets eyes on Maria, he is drawn to her instantly, as she is to him. A cautious, powerful love develops. Maria brings out all Jordan's most tender and passionate desires. He yearns to love and protect her for ever, to take her back to America, yet knows that he may be dead in a matter of days.

The lovers snatch moments of happiness while enemy planes fly overhead. Pilar takes Jordan to visit El Sordo, another guerrilla leader higher up in the mountains, to try to enlist his help. Once again Jordan is in the position of an outsider asking for support for a plan which

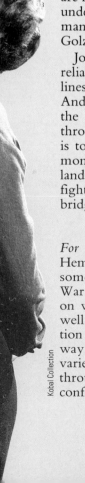

Pilar and the bullfighter
Remembering her love affair with the matador Finito de Palencia (above), Pilar recounts his courage in the ring.

looks dangerously like a suicide mission – but El Sordo agrees.

On the way to El Sordo's camp, Pilar tells the story of Pablo's capture of a town early in the war, and of the atrocities he and his followers committed against the fascists. The graphic details of the brutalities serve to remind them all that there has been barbarism on both sides, yet still this unhappy war must go on.

A snowfall two nights before the bridge is due to be blown spells disaster for El Sordo. Returning from a horse raid, his tracks are followed, and he and his men are ruthlessly wiped out. Jordan begins to understand the full extent of the enemy manoeuvres and the hopelessness of Golz's original plan.

Jordan sends Andrés, one of Pablo's reliable men, back through Republican lines to take a dispatch to the General. Andrés meets obstacles and difficulties all the way, and only just manages to get through to Golz at the last minute. But it is too late to change the orders sent out months before, even though the military landscape has altered. The small brave fighting band must still try to blow up the bridge, and risk their lives for the cause.

A STUDY OF WAR

For Whom the Bell Tolls was born out of Hemingway's determination to record some of the events of the Spanish Civil War. It is essentially a war novel, focusing on what war does to individual lives as well as exposing the extremes of degradation that accompany the killing. Hemingway achieves this by developing richly varied and sympathetic characters through whom the experience of the conflict is made real.

experimenting with untried narrative techniques and letting the characters reveal themselves through their own stories. By ranging back and forth in time, Hemingway managed to convey a sense of an entire life encapsulated in a few brief days – days enriched and informed by past experiences. It is this extraordinary quality which sets this novel above others, and which was to gain Hemingway a Nobel Prize for his 'mastery of the art of modern narration'.

BRUTALITY AND BEAUTY
One of Hemingway's chief concerns in the novel is to lay bare the brutality of war. People on both sides of the conflict are shown at their most bestial, clearly relishing the legitimization of murder. Others, however, are closer to Hemingway's own stance and wrestle with their consciences about the need to kill in the name of the cause.

Pilar's account of Pablo's assault on a small town at the start of the war forms one of the most vivid sequences in the whole novel. Each execution is described in minute detail, bringing the atrocities

Using all the best elements of a journalistic style, Hemingway creates a powerful tension which increases as the hours roll relentlessly on. The language of the novel is simple, sharp and vivid, including much colloquial Spanish to set the scene. Robert Jordan, the clear-thinking, reserved American, is aware all the time of the importance of recording the events around him. He plans to write a book about it all when he returns home, half-knowing he may never have the chance. In the meantime he listens and interprets and marvels at the stories he hears around him, in particular from Pilar: "If that woman could only write . . . God, how she could tell a story."

So rich is the story-telling from Pilar and others that it is hard to believe the action of the novel lasts only three days. Time is distorted in the madness of war. "There is no such thing as a shortness of time . . .", Jordan argues with himself on the morning of the explosion. "I have been all my life in these hills since I have been here." The intensity of those few days among Pablo's people leaves Jordan feeling he has learned more in that brief span than at any other time in his life.

In *For Whom the Bell Tolls*, Hemingway consciously broke new ground,

Alfred East: Algeciras (detail)/Roy Miles Fine Paintings/Bridgeman Art Library

> *"I hope I am not for the killing, Anselmo was thinking. I think that after the war there will have to be some great penance done for the killing. If we no longer have religion after the war then I think there must be some form of civic penance organized that all may be cleansed from the killing or else we will never have a true and human basis for living".*

alive to her audience, Jordan and Maria. Pilar talks in order to share the horror, making the point that the killing takes places on both sides: ". . . I sat there and I did not wish to think for that was the worst day of my life . . ."

A great deal of Jordan's private thoughts centre on his own capacity for killing. Reading through the letters of a young cavalry man he has just shot, Jordan thinks bitterly, "You never kill anyone that you want to kill in a war." Killing must be done as "a necessity but you must not believe in it. If you believe in it the whole thing is wrong".

Another of the band, Anselmo, abhors killing much more than Jordan. A hunter of animals in his old life, he believes the taking of human life is a brutalizing experience. "The killing is necessary, I know, but still the doing of it is very bad for a man and I think that, after all this is over and we have won the war, there must be a penance of some for the cleansing of us all."

Anselmo is the voice of conscience in the novel. He is a diligent, faithful servant of the cause, and his commitment to winning the war against the fascists shines out in the face of so much human failure. His stand is all the more heroic as it becomes clear that the higher ranks in the Republican cause are incompetent.

The contrast between those who control, give orders, abuse and manipulate, and those who carry out actions, suffer, and die, gives the story enormous poignancy. Amid the mess and carnage of the war there are good, ordinary people, who believe in a better future for Spain and are prepared to die anonymous, inglorious deaths for that belief.

Hemingway was fascinated by this aspect of war: the beauty born of brutality, appearing in unexpected places. Robert Jordan stumbles across beautiful, sad, brutalized, orphaned Maria, and falls in love with a passion and intensity he has

In the Background

SPANISH GYPSIES

Pablo and his band are all *gitanos* or gypsies. These nomadic people – of whom there are about 200,000 in Spain today – are believed to have arrived in Europe from India in the late Middle Ages. They are often attributed with supernatural powers and appear in stories as healers or fortune tellers.

A bad omen
The appearance of enemy planes flying overhead (above left) spells danger for the guerrillas. Their untrained bands of fighters, like the gypsies below left, are no match for the military strength of the fascists.

Blowing the bridge
Robert Jordan has been recruited for just one thing – the blowing up of a bridge (right). Whether he succeeds in his mission, and whether he loses his life in the process, hang in the balance.

never before experienced. The irony of the timing is not lost on him:

"And then, on a lousy show like this, co-ordinating two chicken-crut guerrilla bands to help you blow a bridge under impossible conditions . . . you run into a girl like this Maria."

Another kind of beauty celebrated in the novel is the courage of the fighter, especially in overcoming fear. Hemingway makes a parallel between war and bullfighting, as Andrés, the messenger, remembers his years in the bullring, and the relief when it rained and he would not have to fight. Pilar describes the matador Finito, her lover before Pablo: "Finito was afraid all the time and in the ring he was like a lion."

In facing death like a lion there is much beauty. The assault on El Sordo and his men forms one of the most violent and bloody chapters in the book. But among the slaughter of dead horses and dying men is El Sordo, whose last thoughts have a haunting poetic quality:

"Death was nothing and he had no picture of it nor fear of it in his mind. But living was a field of grain blowing in the wind on the side of a hill. Living was a hawk in the sky. Living was an earthen jar of water in the dust of the threshing . . ."

CHARACTERS IN FOCUS

Hemingway uses dialogue as a central device in *For Whom the Bell Tolls*, inserting occasional Spanish phrases to enhance the flavour. From the obscenity-ridden exchanges of Agustín and Pilar to the formalized speech of Jordan and Maria, all the characters reveal themselves in their everyday conversations, not just showing their personalities, but also filling in the dark, rich areas of their past lives.

WHO'S WHO

Robert Jordan Maria's lover, the scholarly American hero who nevertheless "knew how to blow any sort of bridge that you can name".

Pablo The weary guerrilla leader who has lost his appetite for war, and whose cowardice breeds treachery.

Pilar With her "brown face like a model for a granite monument", Pilar is the real leader of Pablo's band, and a passionate supporter of the Republican cause.

Maria Vulnerable, skittish and beautiful, she is a victim of the war and inspires the love and protectiveness of both Jordan and Pilar.

Anselmo The elderly peasant guide whose values and decency win Jordan's trust.

General Golz A brilliant Russian commander, whose scheme it is to blow up the bridge.

Rafael Charming, idle, fun-loving and talkative, he is an ally of Pablo's band.

El Sordo The deaf, veteran guerrilla leader to whom Pilar turns for advice. He is remarkably brave in the face of death.

Agustín A fighter for the cause who loves Maria. "He speaks very filthily and always in jokes but he is a very serious man."

Fernando Another fighter, who is ridiculed for his dullness until his loyalty comes to the fore.

Neil Pinkett

U. Caputo: The Midday Break (detail)/Fine Art Photographic Library

With hair "the golden brown of a grain field that has been burned dark in the sun", Maria (above) is a loved and protected member of Pablo's band. She bears the scars of her past – having been raped and tortured by fascist soldiers – but with Pilar's and Jordan's help the scars are fading. Day by day she grows visibly stronger, more serene and more beautiful.

Treacherous in his cowardice, Pablo (left) is the nominal leader of the gypsies hiding in the mountains. "His eyes were small and set too wide apart and his ears were small and set close to his head." Despite his unreliability, his knowledge of the mountains makes him useful to Jordan, but the *Inglés* recognizes that "this man is bad and he constitutes a danger" to the blowing of the bridge. "From one year of war" Pablo has "become lazy, a drunkard and a coward", his woman Pilar hisses. "Thou hast seen the ruin that now is Pablo", but in the past he was a very different sort of man – cunning and fearless. "Pablo is very intelligent but very brutal", Pilar says, warning Jordan that he is not to be underestimated.

"Tall and thin with sun-streaked fair hair, and a wind- and sun-burned face", Robert Jordan (right) is the handsome, remarkable hero of the story. Both a thinker and a man of action, he has left his safe university post in the United States to fight for the cause of freedom in Spain. "He fought now in this war because it had started in a country that he loved . . . and if it were destroyed life would be unbearable for all those people who believed in it." When Maria unexpectedly enters his world he recognizes that "whether it lasts just through today and a part of tomorrow, or whether it lasts for a long life [it] is the most important thing that can happen to a human being."

Symbol of all that is good and decent, Anselmo (left) is a fighter who abhors the bloodshed. "I think that after the war there will have to be some great penance done for the killing." Without some spiritual cleansing there can be no "true and human basis for living". Childless and often lonely, he nevertheless has one thing "that no man nor any God can take away from me and that is that I worked well for the Republic . . . I have worked my best from the first of the movement and I have done nothing I am ashamed of." The moral voice of the novel, his dedication and sense of honour make him Jordan's most trusted ally.

A marvellous storyteller, Pilar (above) "has a tongue that scalds and that bites like a bull whip. With this tongue she takes the hide from anyone." But there is also an underlying tenderness in her, an honesty and decency that inspire loyalty from all who know her. She is warm and generous, committed to the cause and, unlike Pablo, unafraid. She can read people's palms but if the future looks bad she dismisses it as "all gypsy nonsense that I make to give myself an importance". To Jordan she is "like a mountain", providing a base for young trees to grow tall and strong. But in her own eyes she is ugly: "I was born ugly. All my life I have been ugly." To the many men who have loved her, however, she is beautiful – "much woman".

IN PRAISE OF HEROES

Renowned for the 'machismo' of his heroes, Hemingway combined his muscular realism with an economy of style that made his writing the more powerful for what was left unsaid.

'War groups the maximum of material and speeds up the action and brings out all sorts of stuff that normally you would have to wait a lifetime to get.' In these lines, written to his fellow-novelist Scott Fitzgerald, Hemingway explained his pre-occupation with war and violence by indicating their power to heighten and concentrate experience – a function particularly valuable to a writer. Warfare, or its memory or aftermath, provides the background for most of Hemingway's novels and stories. And when not writing of war, he generally dealt with its peacetime substitutes – intense physical activities such as bullfighting, hunting, boxing, and other sports that tested individuals' courage and endurance.

WRITING FROM EXPERIENCE

All of these things played a great part in Hemingway's own life, and it is hardly surprising to learn that his fiction is closely related to his personal history. The wars, the sports, the places (Milan, Paris, Spain, Key West, Kenya, Cuba, Venice) are much the same in fiction as in fact: and the stoical 'Hemingway hero' usually shares many experiences with his creator

and is often understandably identified with him. Nevertheless Hemingway's intentions were not autobiographical. In his view the writer's material had to be mined from deep personal experience – 'the great reserve of things he knows or has seen' – but the reason was that this was the only basis for successful invention. 'A writer's job is to tell the truth. His standard of fidelity to the truth should be so high that his invention, out of experience, should produce a truer account than anything factual can be.' And so, without really contradicting himself, Hemingway was about to claim that 'Everything good that he'd ever written he'd made up'.

Authentic knowledge, Hemingway

'Goddam wonderful'
Hemingway called Joyce's Ulysses *'a goddam wonderful book' and Joyce (right) admired Hemingway (below) for being 'ready to live the life he writes about'.*

Wild cities
(left) While living in Chicago and Kansas, and working for the Co-operative Commonwealth journal, young Hemingway wrote about big-city crime.

War reporter
Hemingway went to report the Spanish Civil War for the North American Newspaper Alliance, claiming no allegiance to either side, but becoming a champion of the Left.

believed, enabled a writer to strip down and shape his material without any sacrifice of emotional depth. 'I always try to write on the principle of the iceberg. There is seven-eighths of it underwater for every part that shows. Anything you know you can eliminate and it only strengthens your iceberg. It is the part that doesn't show. If a writer omits something because he does not know it then there is a hole in the story.' In other words there is a real, if oblique, connection between experience and literature, and specifically between Hemingway's lifestyle and his literary style and stance.

RUTHLESS PERFECTIONIST

As this suggests, Hemingway's toughguy image concealed a dedicated, thoughtful artist for whom writing was a painstaking and difficult calling. His perfectionism limited his output to a handful of novels, sixty-odd short stories, and four nonfiction works, notably his famous study of bullfighting, *Death in the Afternoon* (1932), an account of a month's safari, *Green Hills of Africa* (1935), and *A Moveable Feast* (1964), containing his memories of Paris in the 1920s. Works that failed to meet his exacting standards were ruthlessly discarded – and these included two long novels, *Islands in the Stream* and *The Garden of Eden*, both of which were posthumously published (1970 and 1986). When finished, his works were subject to heavy cutting. And, on occasion, Hemingway would attack an artistic problem again and again with heroic obstinacy: 'I rewrote the ending to *Farewell to Arms*, the last page of it, thirty-nine times before I was satisfied.'

The celebrated Hemingway style also

resulted from a fusion of authentic experience and scrupulous craftsmanship. Very early in his career Hemingway realized that it was hard to know 'how you truly felt' (not how you were supposed to feel), or exactly what happened in action. It was vital to observe truthfully and record accurately. ('If a writer stops observing he is finished.') And the writer must also be able to identify and use the significant details that brought the action to life – 'the unnoticed things that made emotions,

'The Snows of Kilimanjaro'
The mountain (below) and a preying hyena convince the hero of the sin of frittering away life and talent: a favourite Hemingway theme.

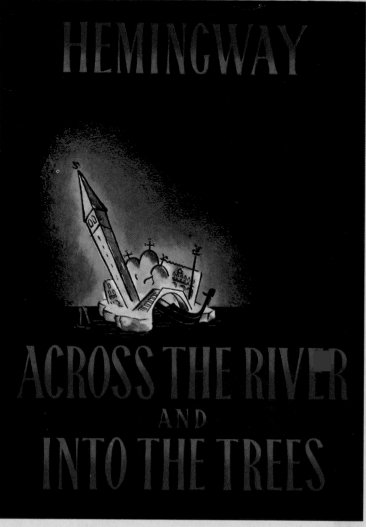

such as . . . the squeak of resin on canvas under a fighter's flat-soled gym shoes'.

One of the distinctive features of Hemingway's work is that feelings and emotional situations are rarely shown directly. They have to be inferred from the action and dialogue of the story, and are therefore felt all the more strongly for their understatement – like the seven-eighths of the iceberg. For this purpose Hemingway's style – apparently simple and colloquial, yet carefully crafted and quite distinctive in tone – was the proper vehicle. Though widely misinterpreted as 'hard-boiled' or 'realistic', it influenced an entire generation of writers from John Steinbeck to Dashiell Hammett and Raymond Chandler.

'GRACE UNDER PRESSURE'

Hemingway's outlook was fundamentally tragic. His world is a violent one in which men struggle against difficult odds, are tested up to or beyond their limits, and have no serious hope of victory. As Frederic Henry, the hero of *A Farewell to Arms,* discovers with bitterness, "That was what you did. You died. You did not know what it was about. You never had time to learn . . . they killed you in the end. You could count on that." But what mattered to Hemingway was not life's tragic end but how a man conducted himself during the struggle. In *The Old Man and the Sea*, Santiago reflects that "A man may be destroyed but not defeated". All Hemingway's work is concerned with 'honour, that outmoded and all-important word' which enables his heroes to exhibit 'grace under pressure'. Corrupt living, unsustained by courage and integrity, is worthless, as Hemingway indicates in the ironic title of a famous story, *The Short Happy Life of Francis Macomber:*

Venetian muse
Adriana Ivancich (above) was model for the Venetian heroine of Across the River and into the Trees. *She illustrated the edition, right, and was an integral part of the author's romance with 'God-damned wonderful' Venice.*

on safari, the sexually humiliated and broken-nerved Macomber experiences a 'short happy life' only for the few minutes between recovering his courage and being shot by the wife who has preyed on his weakness.

RIGHTING WRONGS

Hemingway's fiction is mainly concerned with the plight of the individual in a hostile universe, and the early *In Our Time* (1925), like the late *Across the River and into the Trees* (1950), portrays war as a disillusioning experience. But in the 1930s, the Great Depression and the rise of fascism prompted Hemingway to unexpected commitments. The dying hero of *To Have and Have Not* (1937) realizes that "a man alone ain't got no . . . chance". And the much more successful *For Whom the Bell Tolls* (1940) owes its title to a sermon which warns that every man's fate concerns his fellow-men – and, as the use of the quotation by Hemingway implied, that victory for

fascism in Spain would threaten freedom everywhere. Never did he more completely justify his stated belief that 'great writing comes out of a sense of injustice'.

Student of his craft
Despite his image of rough-cut brawler, Hemingway (right) wrote, and experimented with styles of writing, with great seriousness.

Ernest Hemingway's first collection of stories, *In Our Time* (1925), shows his characteristic preoccupation with action, integrity and 'grace under pressure'; it also introduces his single most famous character, the autobiographical Nick Adams. Hemingway's spare, apparently straightforward style helped to make popular successes of his first two novels, *Fiesta* (or *The Sun Also Rises*) (1926), about Anglo-Saxon expatriates in the Europe of the 1920s, and *A Farewell to Arms* (1929), based on his harrowing experiences during World War I. In the more socially conscious 1930s, he wrote *To Have and Have Not* (1937), contrasting wealth with poverty, crime with 'legitimacy'; and *For Whom the Bell Tolls* (1940) draws heavily on his own involvement in World War I and Spain.

In *The Old Man and the Sea* (1952) it is a humble fisherman who embodies the qualities Hemingway most admired – uncomplaining endurance and outright refusal to ever admit defeat.

T. Moran: Grand Canyon of the Yellowstone. US Department of Interior/Bridgeman Art Library

Pedro Vega y Munoz: The Picador (detail)/Fine Art Photographic Library

IN OUR TIME

✦ 1925 ✦

Among the woods and waters of the Great Outdoors (above), Nick Adams comes to manhood. The most celebrated among this first (and probably best) collection of Hemingway's short stories concern this semi-autobiographical youth, confronting the harsh facts of life. In *Indian Camp*, for example, Nick helps his doctor father deliver an Indian woman's baby – a harrowing experience, at the end of which they discover that her husband, lying in the bunk above, has quietly cut his throat. Each of the 15 stories is prefaced by a brief, superficially unrelated sketch which, together, serve to bind the separate stories into a thematic whole.

In the final story, *Big Two-Hearted River,* an older, war-damaged Nick is healed by contact with the scenes of his boyhood.

FIESTA

✦ 1927 ✦

The physical grace and bravery of Romero the bull-fighter (left) briefly impinge on the lives of a group of cynical, hard-drinking, directionless expatriates in this book (published as *The Sun Also Rises* in 1926) about the post-War 'lost generation' of Americans. The action is seen through the eyes of Jake Barnes, a newspaper correspondent in Paris. His impotence has frustrated a love affair with the beautiful Lady Brett Ashley, now a drifting, listless sophisticate. Brett, her fiancé Mike, Jake and friends go to Spain for the fiesta at Pamplona, where Brett falls in love with Romero. Jake and Mike accept the situation stoically, but not so the novelist Robert Cohn, with whom Brett has a brief affair. The group disperses, and it is only later that Jake learns the outcome of Brett's affair.

93

A FAREWELL TO ARMS

→ 1929 ←

The brutal chaos of World War I (above) pervades this famous novel. Frederic Henry, an American lieutenant in the Italian ambulance service, falls in love with an English nurse, Catherine Barkley. She becomes pregnant, and Henry is caught up in the panic-stricken retreat after Caporetto. He decides to desert and rows Catherine across to neutral Switzerland, but their escape to peace proves illusory.

TO HAVE AND HAVE NOT

→ 1937 ←

In Florida's Key West, Harry Morgan charters his boat (left) to wealthy fishermen, in an effort to support his family. Hit by the Depression and cheated by a client, Harry turns to crime. After a gun-battle with the FBI, he loses his arm and his boat is confiscated. Now he must resort to desperate measures if he is to survive.

ACROSS THE RIVER AND INTO THE TREES
✦ 1950 ✦

Colonel Richard Cantwell returns to the city of Venice (left) that he once helped to defend as a young volunteer in World War I. Now he is a 50-year-old professional soldier whose integrity has prevented him rising to the upper ranks of the US army. He embarks on a bitter-sweet affair with a 19-year-old contessa, knowing that his heart is rapidly giving out. Amid lovingly described Venetian scenes, Cantwell purges himself of harsh memories. Only one last lonely battle remains.

The title is based on the last words of the American general Stonewall Jackson.

THE OLD MAN AND THE SEA
✦ 1952 ✦

Santiago, a poor Cuban fisherman (below), has gone 84 days without taking a fish and is now regarded as *saloa*, 'the worst form of unlucky'. He has even lost the services of the boat-boy Manolin whose parents have sent him to work on a luckier boat. Manolin loves Santiago, however, and surreptitiously helps and feeds him. On the 85th day, Santiago tries to change his luck by rowing his skiff far out into the sea. There he hooks a fish so big that it tows him still farther out. And the struggle to the death is only just beginning. This brief moral fable played a major role in winning Hemingway the 1954 Nobel Prize.

**When civil war ripped Spain apart, extraordinary heroism
mingled, like the blood in the gutters, with atrocities
engendered by bigotry, ambition and senseless slaughter.**

During the late 1930s, politically aware people were forced to take sides in a confused and confusing struggle, a struggle that in its origins at least had nothing to do with anyone but the Spanish. According to individual perceptions (or prejudices), the Spanish Civil War was either a gallant struggle to preserve the fledgling Spanish Republic from the fascist menace, or it was a crusade to defend order and Christianity from the threat of Communism. As such, it crystallized the most heated political debate of the period.

For outsiders it was probably necessary to take a simplified view of the conflict because it was extremely complicated. At its roots were antagonisms unique to Spain: the particular nature of the class system and attempts to overhaul it, the role of the Catholic Church, the discrepancy between the Castilian heartland and the more advanced Basque provinces and Catalonia.

The war was triggered by a military conspiracy

Workers unite!
*The civil war in Spain
split the nation and
polarized most of Europe.
Republican propaganda
viewed the Nationalist
rebels as 'foreign' invaders
menacing the self-
determination of the
Spanish people, and
appealed to its neighbours,
for help. The posters
below cry, 'Spain fights
for its independence, for
peace and solidarity
among all peoples', and
call on the workers of
France to rally to the
cause.*

against the Government, a liberal régime which depended on the support of a miscellany of socialists and a small, but growing Communist Party. This Popular Front, as it was called, had emerged as the most viable political grouping following the deposition of the Monarchy in 1931. But by 1936, it was in severe difficulty because of its own economic incompetence and because it was unable to stem the tide of political sabotage and violence – mainly perpetrated by anarchist elements in the labour movement.

On the other side of the political divide were ranged powerful opponents of the democratic experiment. Right-wing military men had come to believe that chaos was imminent, and that out of such chaos would come a revolution similar to that of 1917 in Russia. The political right generally shared that analysis, which of course was anathema to them. On the whole, the Church and the middle classes were increasingly pessimistic about the prospects of Spanish democracy, while die-hard royalists and the semi-fascist Falange movement were its avowed enemies.

FRANCO'S GRAND PLAN
The military conspiracy came to fruition on 18 July 1936, when the able young general Francisco Franco flew in secret from the Canary Islands to Spanish Morocco, to take command of 24,000 disaffected troops. Taking the action as a signal for a general uprising of the Right, the overall strategy was straightforward. Franco would consolidate his control of Spanish Morocco, which he accomplished easily, and then transport his Army of Africa to southern Spain. His principal co-conspirator, General Emilio Mola, would mobilize the troops under his command in northern Spain. Together they would move on the centre of the country and Madrid. Given Madrid's special significance as the emotional, as well as governmental, centre of Spain, a quick victory there might well have given the whole war to the rebels.

As with most grand strategies, the practical execution of this plan proved stubbornly difficult. There were immediate, widespread mutinies in garrisons, and within days the north-west of Spain, Navarre and parts of central Spain were in rebel hands. Individual cities in the south (princi-

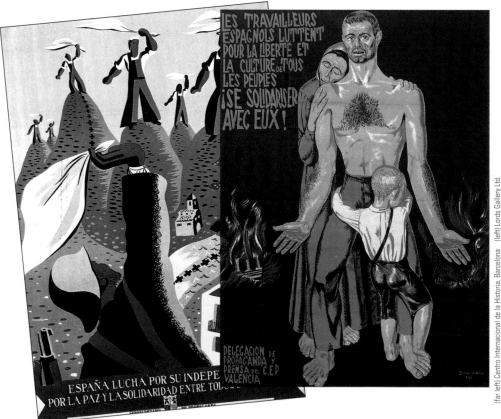

ES TRAVAILLEURS ESPAGNOLS LUTTENT POUR LA LIBERTÉ ET LA CULTURE DE TOUS LES PEUPLES ¡SE SOLIDARISER AVEC EUX!

DELEGACION DE PROPAGANDA Y PRENSA DEL C.E.P. VALENCIA

ESPAÑA LUCHA POR SU INDEPE... POR LA PAZ Y LA SOLIDARIDAD ENTRE TO...

pally Seville, Granada and Cordoba) came out for the rebels, who also controlled the Canaries and Majorca as well as Spanish Morocco. But, critically, the Government was able to quell army dissidents in Madrid and Barcelona, and most of central, southern and eastern Spain entered the struggle on the Government's side.

Instead of a relatively simple military takeover, then, the struggle for Spain became a full-scale civil war. It is a historical truism that civil wars are peculiarly horrible, the reason being that they introduce a personal note that is absent in other conflicts. They provide the opportunity to pay off old scores, unleashing in the process the very darkest forces of the human psyche. There were plenty of old scores to settle in Spain, and, from the outset, the conduct of the Spanish Civil War was marked by a savage brutality that sickened the rest of the world.

Hemingway does not shy away from this, and Pilar's mercilessly detailed account of Pablo's nonchalant shooting of the civil guards, followed by the orgy of killing in the town, is truly chilling. The incident may be fictional, but the barbarous behaviour it describes is not. And it occurred on both sides. Twelve bishops and thousands of priests and nuns were slaughtered in the name of the Republic. In one province of Aragon, 80 per

Early advances
General Francisco Franco (above centre) caught Spain between sharp jaws: military mutinies in his favour in the North and his invasion forces (top right) pushing up from the South. The poorly armed, disorganized and schismatic Republicans did not appear to stand a chance, and suffered severe casualties (above). The photo, top left, of a Republican at the moment of death was published in Life *magazine and was an image which fired much sympathy abroad.*

cent of the priests were killed. The Nationalists (as the rebels called themselves) instituted a deadly witch-hunt in the areas under their control, and summarily shot an estimated 50,000 leftist sympathizers. After Badajoz fell to the Nationalists in August 1936, something like 1800 men (and apparently some women too) were paraded into the bullring, arms in the air, to be mowed down by machine guns.

PROVING GROUND
From the beginning, the Spanish Civil War also took on an international dimension. The Nationalists appealed to Fascist Italy and Nazi Germany for help, which was readily forthcoming. Mussolini despatched the first of nearly 800 Italian aircraft, and by the end of the conflict at least 50,000 Italian troops were serving in Spain. Hitler was also eager to help the cause, and sent transport planes to airlift Franco's Moroccan forces to the mainland. For Goering, the war was the perfect opportunity 'to test my young Luftwaffe'. German war materials, technicians, pilots and tank crews continued to enter Spain throughout the war, in relatively small numbers but to great effect. Spain was to serve as a 'dress rehearsal' for World War II.

The Republicans, or Loyalists as they came to

be known, whom Hemingway supported, appealed to the western democracies, in particular neighbouring France. The French were sympathetic and at first provided some planes and weapons, but then backed off when it became apparent that the British were determined not to get involved. The French did, however, gain British support for an international agreement banning arms sales to both sides. The Italians and Germans cynically agreed to this and then ignored it.

The Loyalists did get tangible support from Soviet Russia which, like Italy and Germany, had only paid lip-service to the policy of non-intervention. Russian assistance comprised planes, guns and tanks, and perhaps 2000 soldiers. The clandestine nature of the Russian involvement is starkly illustrated by Hemingway in the matter of the three wounded Russians, who were to be murdered and stripped in the event of the Loyalist forces having to evacuate Madrid.

THE INTERNATIONAL BRIGADES
More important, in the context of *For Whom the Bell Tolls,* was the international Communist movement, directed from Moscow, which set up and commanded the famed International Brigades. These attracted volunteers from all over Europe, the United States and Canada, the majority of whom (but not all) were Communists or Communist sympathizers. The English writer George Orwell, for example, although not a Communist, fought with Trotskyist groups in Catalonia. Hemingway's American hero, Robert Jordan, is likewise not a Communist, but he is very willing to serve under Russian command because he admires their discipline and their military competence. In all, some 45,000 men bore arms in the International Brigades, including 3000 of Robert Jordan's compatriots. By contrast, only a handful of volunteers from the democracies saw fit to join up with the Nationalist forces.

Ideal encouragement
Ernest Hemingway, pictured above with members of the International Brigade, was one of the celebrated sympathizers drafted in to encourage Loyalist fighters.

Barcelona falls
Leftist factions had slaughtered each other, and Republican refugees had massed there, before non-stop bombing by Italian planes gave Barcelona (right) into Nationalist hands.

So it was that long-standing Spanish enmities boiled over into a miniature European war, between the forces of Communism and fascism. This ideological dimension is clearly expressed in the novel's language, where the combatants routinely label all their opponents as fascists and all their allies as Reds.

By September 1936, Italian and German airpower had allowed Franco to brave the Loyalist navy and transport his Army of Africa to Algeciras. The long march on Madrid began, while Mola moved southward. To Mola is credited a phrase that would long outlive him (in fact he died in a plane crash early in the war), when he replied to the question, which of his four columns would take Madrid, 'The Fifth Column'. By that he meant secret sympathizers inside Madrid.

AT THE BARRICADES

By the end of October 1936, Franco was outside Madrid, and it seemed to the world that the Loyalist cause was lost. On 6 November the Government transferred to Valencia, and the following day the Nationalists entered Madrid. They encountered a militia and civilian population determined to fight them street by street, and such was the dread inspired by the Badajoz massacre that women and children set to the building of barricades. On 8 November, 2000 men of the International Brigades, well-armed with Russian equipment, finally reached beleaguered Madrid, and this stiffened the resistance. Decisively, Loyalist lines held when the Nationalists reached the university in the heart of the city. The fighting here became a byword for heroic resistance to fascism, with eye-witness accounts of such desperate improvisation as building barricades 'with volumes of Indian metaphysics and 19th century German philosophy – quite bullet-proof'!

The Nationalists made repeated attempts to subdue Madrid until the end of March 1937. Then, accepting that it was stalemate for the time

being, Franco turned his attention to the North of Spain, although Madrid remained under a siege of varying intensity to the bitter end. In the north, Franco (now the undisputed leader of Nationalist Spain) made steady headway. The Basque capital Bilbao fell on 19 June 1937, and by the end of that year the whole of northern Spain was under Nationalist control.

THE TRAGEDY OF GUERNICA

During the Basque campaign, there occurred an event that caused an international outcry at the time, and one that half a century later has lost none of its potency as a symbol of military atrocity: the bombing of Guernica.

Guernica was a little market town with a population of about 7000, lying 18 miles to the east of Bilbao. Monday, 26 April, like all Mondays, was market day, and the streets and main square were busy with the traffic and trade of neighbouring farmers and townsfolk. At 4.30 p.m. a peal of bells rang out to announce an air raid. Ten minutes later a wave of German Heinkel bombers appeared overhead, bombed the plaza and then machine-gunned the streets. The terrified people tried to flee the town, as fresh waves of Junker 52s reinforced the message of the Heinkels, dropping huge incendiary bombs and high explosives, and raking the panic-ridden streets with machine-gun fire. By 8 p.m. the raid was over, leaving Guernica littered with dead and wounded. How many died has never been satisfactorily established, but the figure often quoted is 1600, with another 900 wounded. At least 70 per cent of the town's buildings were completely destroyed.

Even if the figure for deaths is exaggerated, the survivors' description of the carnage was horrific. One witness claimed to see a crowd of women and children in the plaza blown high into the air, where 'they started to break up. Legs, arms, heads, and bits and pieces flying everywhere'.

The Nationalists immediately tried to mini-

Guernica
The ancient Basque capital, Guernica, swarmed with refugees and retreating Republican soldiers on the day German planes bombed it to extinction. So great was the outcry that even Germany regretted their strategy. Painter Pablo Picasso immortalized the massacre (left).

Women's war
As the war grew more desperate, many women took up guns in the Republican cause (right).

mize the propaganda damage by disclaiming responsibility (on behalf of the Germans). They suggested, lamely, that the Basques themselves had dynamited their own town, in order to facilitate their retreat (Guernica was a road and rail junction). In fact, the overwhelming evidence suggests that the Germans chose Guernica, a marginal military target, as a testing ground for so-called saturation civilian bombing. And while the world would soon witness and experience far more and far worse, this would not blur the image of devastated Guernica. Picasso's master-piece of that name has ensured its immortality.

THE FALL OF BARCELONA

During 1938 the war dragged on, while all the time the prospects for the Loyalists weakened. They lost Teruel in February (having taken it the previous December), and then in April Franco mounted an offensive which swept eastward to the Mediterranean and split the Loyalists. In October, the Nationalists broke through the line of the river Ebro, and then on 26 January 1939 they entered a refugee-packed Barcelona, unopposed.

Half a million refugees fled to France, along with the Loyalist government, and this signalled the end of the war. On 27 February 1939, Britain and France recognized Franco's government, even though Madrid, where remnants of the Loyalist government remained, continued its stubborn resistance. But this collapsed amid bitter infight-ing between Communists and elected Republicans, and on 28 March 1939 Franco took the exhausted, starving capital, unopposed. At a cost of 600,000 lives, the war that was to be described as a dress-rehearsal for the greater one to come, was over.

The final toll
Half a million refugees fled Spain (right). Republican Madrid held out until starved and shelled into submission. Then thousands of those who had given the Nationalists their hardest struggle paid for their obstinacy with their lives (below).

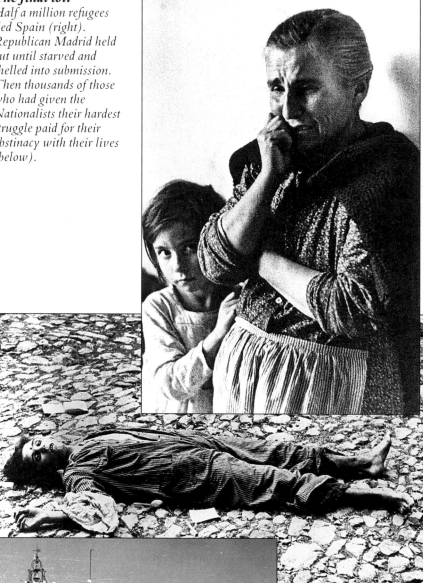

Robert Capa/John Hillelson Agency

BBC Hulton Picture Library

Weidenfeld Archive

Ruthless victory
When Franco's troops took Madrid (left) the war was over. But the dying was not. Republican troops trapped at the coast and unable to escape capture, leapt into the sea. And it is said that more reprisal killings and 'executions' followed the Civil War than took place during it.

100

BIBLIOGRAPHY

Armstrong, Louis, *Satchmo: My Life in New Orleans.* Da Capo Press (Jersey City, 1986)

Benson, Jackson J., *The True Adventures of John Steinbeck, Writer: A Biography.* Viking Penguin (New York, 1984)

Berg, Scott A., *Max Perkins.* Washington Square Press (New York, 1983)

Bernstein, Irving, *A Caring Society: The New Deal, the Worker and the Great Depression.* Houghton Mifflin (Boston, 1985)

Brian, Denis, *The True Gen: An Intimate Portrait of Hemingway by Those Who Knew Him.* Grove Press (New York, 1987)

Bruccoli, Matthew J., *Some Sort of Epic Grandeur: The Life of F. Scott Fitzgerald.* Harcourt Brace Jovanovich (San Diego, 1981)

Burgess, Anthony, *Ernest Hemingway and His World.* Charles Scribner (New York 1985)

Buttitta, Tony, *The Lost Summer: A Personal Memoir of F. Scott Fitzgerald.* St Martin's Press (New York, 1987)

Cameron, Barbara, *Mississippi River.* St Martin's Press (New York, 1987)

Cooper, Stephen, *The Politics of Ernest Hemingway.* UMI Research Press (Ann Arbor, 1987)

Daniels, Roger, *The Bonus March: An Episode of the Great Depression.* Greenwood Press (Westport, 1971)

Emerson, Everett, *The Authentic Mark Twain: A Literary Biography of Samuel L. Clemens.* University of Pennsylvania Press (Philadelphia, 1985)

Enright, R. T., *Capone's Chicago.* Northstar Maschek (Lakeville, 1987)

French, Warren, *John Steinbeck.* G. K. Hall (Boston, 1984)

Fuentes, Norberto, *Hemingway in Cuba.* Lyle Stuart (Secaucus, 1984)

Gallo, Rose A., *F. Scott Fitzgerald.* Ungar Publishing (New York, 1984)

Gandy, Joan W., ed., *The Mississippi Steamboat Era in Historic Photographs.* Dover Publications (New York, 1987)

Gregory, Walter, *The Shallow Grave: A Memoir of the Spanish Civil War.* David & Charles (North Pomfret, 1987)

Hotchner, A. E., *Papa Hemingway: The Ecstasy and Sorrow.* William Morrow (New York, 1983)

Hurt, R. Douglas, *The Dust Bowl.* Nelson-Hall (Chicago, 1981)

Kiernan, Thomas, *The Intricate Music: A Biography of John Steinbeck.* Little, Brown (Boston, 1979)

Kyvig, David E., *Repealing National Prohibition.* University of Chicago Press (Chicago, 1980)

Leacock, Stephen, *Mark Twain.* Haskell Booksellers (Brooklyn, 1974)

Leuchtenberg, William E., *Franklin D. Roosevelt and the New Deal.* Harper & Row (New York, 1963)

Martinez, Raymond J., *Portraits of New Orleans Jazz.* Pelican (Gretna, 1971)

McElvaine, Robert S., *The Great Depression: America, 1929-1941.* Times Books (New York, 1985)

McLane, Merrill F., *Proud Outcasts: The Gypsies of Spain.* Carderock Press (Cabin John, 1987)

Mellow, James R., *Charmed Circle: Gertrude Stein and Company.* Avon Books (New York, 1982)

Mellow, James R., *Invented Lives: The Marriage of F. Scott and Zelda Fitzgerald.* Houghton Mifflin (Boston, 1984)

Milford, Nancy, *Zelda.* Harper & Row (New York, 1983)

Miller, Robert K., *Mark Twain.* Ungar Publishing (New York, 1983)

Morrow, Patrick, *Bret Harte.* Boise State University (Boise, 1972)

Owens, Louis, *John Steinbeck's Re-Vision of America.* University of Georgia Press (Athens, 1985)

Parish, Peter, *The American Civil War.* Holmes & Meier (New York, 1975)

Payne, Stanley G., *The Franco Regime.* University of Wisconsin Press (Madison, 1987)

Phillips, Gene, *Fiction, Film and F. Scott Fitzgerald.* Loyola University Press (Chicago, 1986)

Smith, Gene, *The Shattered Dream: Herbert Hoover and the Great Depression.* McGraw-Hill (New York, 1984)

Whelan, Richard, *Robert Capa: A Biography.* Ballantine Books (New York, 1986)

Zall, Paul M., ed., *Mark Twain Laughing: Humorous Anecdotes by and about Samuel L. Clemens.* University of Tennessee Press (Knoxville, 1987)

INDEX